Grief Denied

A Vietnam Widow's Story

Pauline Laurent
211 A Stony Point Road
Santa Rosa, CA 95401

Published by Catalyst For Change
P.O. Box 5158
Santa Rosa, CA 95402

Grateful acknowledgement for permission to reprint the following:
Page 20, and page 63 from The Prophet, © Kahlil Gibran, 1923. Used
by permission of Alfred A. Knopf, Inc. Publisher of Borzoi Books, 201
East 50th Street, NY, NY 10022
Page 75, from Dialogues with a Modern Mystic © Andrew Harvey and
Mark Matousek 1994. Used by permission of The Theosophical
Publishing House, P.O. Box 270, Wheaton, IL 60189-0270
Page 94, from Healing Rain © Kirtana, © 1990. Used by permission
of Wild Dove Music, P.O. Box 221861, Carmel, CA 93922
Page 116, from All My Life, by Karla Bonhoff © 1986 Seagrape Music.
Used by permission. All rights reserved.
Page 125, from Achilles in Vietnam © Jonathan Shay, 1994. Used by
permission of Scribner, a Division of Simon & Schuster Inc. 1633
Broadway, NY, NY 10019
Page 131, from Love in Action: Writings on Nonviolent Social Change
© Thich Nhat Hahn, 1993. Used by permission of Parallax Press,
Berkeley, CA 94707
Page 141, from Johnny's Song © Steve Mason, 1986. Used by permission
of Steve Mason.

ISBN 0-9671424-0-7

Library of Congress Catalog Card Number 99-93155

Book design by Carol Fussell
Cover photo: Howard Querry, Pauline Laurent

Printed in the United States of America

Disclaimer

Writing this book was an instrument of healing and self-discovery for me. Publishing it is a commitment to support others in resolving any denied grief they may have. This book contains solely my personal experiences and observations. It is not my intent to demean or diminish any person, organization or institution.

For Michelle

J ust as it takes a village to raise a child, it takes a community to write a book. Without the help and support of the following people, I could not have written this book. I am grateful…

To Clara Rosemarda, my writing teacher, who one day asked me to write about the thing I was most afraid of – Vietnam.

To Patti Breitman, an extraordinary woman, who supported me in bringing this book to life.

To all the Vietnam Veterans who opened their hearts to me and were willing to listen to my story.

To Charlie and Ann Harootunian, who sponsored my trip to the Vietnam Veterans Memorial and whose support for this book has never waned.

To fellow writers in my writing groups who listened, gave valuable feedback, and encouraged me to continue writing.

To Kerry Granshaw, my editor, who treated my manuscript as if it were a precious child she wanted to help mature, yet not influence too much.

To all my sponsors, sponsorees and members of my 12-step groups who courageously face their addictions and continue to walk through the pain underlying those addictions.

To Gudrun Zomerland, my therapist, who listened to me cry for six years and <u>never, ever,</u> told me to "get over it." Without the container she provided I might not have been able to heal as thoroughly as I have.

To Pearl Laurent, my mother, for all her prayers to St. Jude.

To Michelle, my daughter, who although skeptical at times, encouraged me to listen to, and follow my heart.

And to Howard, my husband, whose relentless love for me softened my heart and allowed me to fall in love with him.

Table of Contents

Prologue

It's a beautiful Sunday afternoon in May – Mother's Day, 1968. Spring in the Midwest is sprouting with life and possibility. The peonies are shooting stalks through the rich, black soil in the flower beds. After morning mass at St. Joseph's, I am sitting in the shade of the big sycamore in Mom's backyard.

My husband, Howard, has been in Vietnam since March. He thought it would be best for me to stay with my parents while he was gone. Princess, our black German shepherd, is my constant companion. She lies at my feet as I glance through the Sunday paper. I notice wedding announcements, department store sales, ads for restaurants, and upcoming movies.

Nestled in the back pages of a remote section of the paper, I spot an article about a battle in Vietnam. I avoid reading about the war, but this article found me. The action described in the article involves Howard's unit – 3rd Battalion, 39th Regiment, 9th Infantry Division.

War Refugees Are Flooding into Saigon

…The Command Post is in a Buddhist pagoda, 20 yards from a tiny Catholic church which serves as the medical aid station. "They hit us hard all last night with mortars and rockets," said Maj. Boone. "Two soldiers from Alpha Company held out during a three-hour attack on

a little bridge across a feeder canal. I don't even know their names but they are up for the Silver Star. We've been lucky so far – only four killed and 14 wounded in the battalion."

Howard is dead. I know it. I don't know how I know, I just know. I can't breathe. Tears are coming. I'm trembling inside and out. Mom comes out into the yard and asks, "What's wrong?"

I show her the article and whisper, "Howard is dead."

Three days later – May 15, 1968

The potatoes fry in their usual pool of lard, lard rendered from the hogs my uncles and brothers slaughter every January. Mom stands over the stove, stirring the potatoes and turning the blood sausage frying in an adjacent skillet.

Princess greets me after I return from my job at Scott Air Force Base. My father sits in his favorite chair, watching the evening news and waiting for dinner to be served.

Something draws me to the front windows. An ugly green sedan with the words "U.S. Army" printed on the side of the door is parked in front of the house. Two men in uniform sit inside the car, looking down at the paperwork on their laps.

The room starts spinning, my hearing becomes muffled, reality is slipping away from me. Princess barks as Mom walks to the front window to see what's causing the commotion.

They're coming to tell me he is dead.

"Please God, let him be wounded, not dead," I say.

The men continue to sit in the car. Hours seem to pass before they get out, straighten their uniforms, and head toward my door. I put Princess in the basement – she doesn't welcome strangers. I come back to open the door and see two men standing before me with the same terror in their eyes that I'm feeling inside of me.

"Good evening," they say, as they remove their hats. "We're looking for Pauline Querry."

"That's me."

They look at my protruding abdomen which holds my unborn child, and then look at each other in silence that lingers too long.

"Was he wounded or killed? How bad is it?"

More silence. Finally they begin.

"We regret to inform you that your husband, Sergeant Howard E. Querry, was fatally wounded on the afternoon of May 10 by a penetrating missile wound to his right shoulder."

I'm dizzy. I can't think straight.

"Dead? Is he dead?"

They don't answer me. They just reread their script as if practicing their lines for a performance they'll give someday.

Grief Denied

"We regret to inform you…"

The room is spinning. I can't think, I can't hear anything. I'm going to faint. Alone… I must be alone to sort this out. Leave me alone.

Instead, I sit politely as they inform me of the details… funeral… remains… escort… military cemetery… medals.

Finally they gather their papers and leave. I politely show them to the door. My parents are hysterical. My dad weeps, my mom trembles. No sound is coming out – her whole body is shaking in upheaval.

After retrieving my dog, I stagger to my room and shut the door. I throw myself on the bed, gasping for air. My heart races and pounds. My unborn baby starts kicking and squirming. I hold my dog with one hand, my baby with the other, and I sob. I'm shattered, blown to pieces. It can't be true.

No medics come, no helicopters fly me away to an emergency room. I struggle to save myself but I cannot. I die.

Half an hour later, a ghost of my former self gets up off the bed and begins planning Howard's funeral.

Mom calls relatives. People come over to console me. I just want to be alone. I just want to be alone.

1. Remembering ...

I t's Fall again – my favorite time of year. Autumn leaves crackle underfoot and the bold harvest moon awakens a longing in me that reminds me of the one and only marriage I ever had.

I promised to love, honor and obey back in September of '67. I gave myself completely to Howard even as I thought, "Until death do us part is a long time. How can I promise to do anything until I die?"

As it turned out, it wasn't such a long time. The following May, only nine months after our wedding, I followed his coffin, draped with the U.S. flag, down the aisle at St. Joseph's Catholic Church, the same aisle I had walked down as a bride. I wore a black maternity dress and felt a life stirring inside me.

The possibility of his death wasn't something Howard and I had talked about, even though it haunted each of us. When we got married he was in the Non-Commissioned Officer Candidate (NCOC) Academy, a training ground for sergeants headed for Vietnam.

I entered the marriage naively. I was in love with my college sweetheart and when he wanted to consummate our love before he went to Vietnam, I agreed. We were invincible. His tour of duty in Vietnam only meant our dreams would be postponed for a year. After all, it was his duty to serve his country just as his father had done during WWII.

Grief Denied

Throughout his training, he knew he was going to Vietnam, but he never told me – until he got his orders. He kept giving me hope – telling me that the administration guarantee he received when he enlisted in the Army was going to come through.

When he got his draft induction notice he immediately went to see an Army recruiter who promised him that if he enlisted, he'd be guaranteed a job in administration – he'd never be in combat. I still have the certificate guaranteeing him an administration job. It's in the envelope along with his death certificate.

When I missed my menstrual cycle during the first month of our marriage, I didn't think much about it. I had always had irregular cycles and after a lengthy series of lab tests, had been told by a gynecologist that I couldn't get pregnant unless I had major surgery. I postponed the surgery because we weren't planning to begin a family until after he returned from Vietnam.

The second month of our marriage when my breasts started enlarging, Howard insisted I go for a pregnancy test, "Honey, just think, you might be pregnant. Wouldn't that be neat?"

The day they told me my test was positive, I drove home in a daze. How could I possibly be pregnant?

Everything was happening too fast – our engagement, our marriage, and now our pregnancy. I felt certain Howard was going to Vietnam and I wondered how I'd manage having a baby by myself.

Howard was delighted with the news of the pregnancy. He wanted a whole house full of "curtain climbers" as he called them. He thought possibly he could postpone going to Vietnam until after the baby was born. I think he was deluding himself as well as me. He knew he was going to Vietnam but thought if he tried hard enough, perhaps he could turn the tides of fate. I sometimes wonder if he had a sense that he'd die in Vietnam and wanted to leave me with his child.

When he graduated from the NCOC Academy, he got orders for Fort Jackson, South Carolina. I was relieved. That gave us a little more time together. At Fort Jackson, he was an acting squad leader with ten men under him. His daily routine was long and grueling; however, he never talked about it. Sometimes in the middle of the night in a frenzied dream, he'd poke me in the back and scream, "Get your rifle."

Twenty-six years after Howard died, Bill Jones, who was in the NCOC Academy with him, told me that on the last day of their Escape and Evasion training, the instructors took all the trainees into a room and said:

> *See the guy on your right, he's not coming back.*
> *See the guy on your left, he's going to be injured.*
> *Now look at yourself – you're coming back.*

The guys who were captured in the Escape and Evasion training were taken to a make-believe POW camp. They were tortured. Bill said, "We could hear them screaming." The ones who gave in and leaked information were marched up on a stage in front of the rest of the trainees and humiliated.

"See these guys – they're the ones you can't trust."

Bill said that whole scene created a great deal of turmoil among the troops. I don't know how Howard endured it all and kept it to himself. The cost of experiencing these and similar experiences, I believe, is at the root of the psychological damage still haunting men who served in that war.

I soon became disillusioned with being an Army wife. I tried to find a job, but since we were military and I was pregnant, no one would hire me. They knew we'd be shipping out soon. So I spent my time fixing up our little rented house with what little money we had, and cooking meals, most of which he missed because he was at the base late every night.

Sometimes on weekends, we had Saturday evening and all day Sunday to ourselves. When this happened we usually went to the NCO club for dinner on Saturday night. It was inexpensive – $3.00 for soup/salad, an entrée and dessert. Howard would always order steak and I'd have some kind of seafood. On Sundays we'd sleep late, take Princess for a walk, and when the weather was nice, we'd wash and wax our new '67 Chevy Nova Coupe.

We had so little time together.

When I met Howard in the summer of '65 we were both working at a bank in Oak Brook, Illinois – a western suburb of Chicago. After my freshman year at Southern Illinois University in Carbondale, Kathy Keenan, one of my roommates, invited me to live with her for the summer. She assured me I'd find a good job. I jumped at the opportunity. My mother wasn't too thrilled that I was going to the big city of Chicago, but she accepted it. She had to.

Soon after I moved in with Kathy and her parents, I walked into the Bank of Oak Brook and applied for a job as secretary to the Vice President. It was a small bank with about eight tellers and four officers. When they asked me if I'd be staying in the area for awhile I said, "Of course." A few days later I began working there. I was 19 years old and excited about the summer ahead of me.

It wasn't long before Howard Emerson Querry, III (his placard read), Head Teller at the bank, began flirting with me and asking me to have lunch with him. He was handsome with a broad smile, perfect teeth, and flawless olive skin. He looked like Frank Sinatra and carried himself confidently. Skinny, yet very sexy, he was sophisticated compared to the young men I'd known in high school. Howard drove a '63 white Ford Fairlane convertible with red interior and smoked one Winston after another. He was only a year older than me, but he'd had a much broader range of experience.

He had a rather wild and reckless nature. His father told me when he was a senior in high school in Miami Beach, he burned out the clutch on the family Cadillac by racing it up and down the beaches in the sand.

Howard presented a mild-mannered, Clark-Kent type of appearance, but underneath was a man who was very passionate about life and hadn't yet learned how to harness that passion.

After a few lunch dates, he invited me over to meet his parents who lived in Downers Grove. They had a sprawling brick home with a rose garden in the back yard. Howard's father was a dentist who specialized in oral surgery. His mother was the dental assistant in the office. On weekends Howard would often invite me to Saturday evening dinner which was held in their formal dining room. Their table was set just like the ones I had seen in my high school Home Economics textbook. My family didn't have a formal dining room when I was growing up. We ate in the kitchen and the utensils, a fork and knife, were often thrown on the table by whoever was designated as the person to set the table that night.

Dr. Querry has the same sense of humor as his son, so when the two of them were together they were constantly trying to out-do each other. Dr. Querry was also an incessant smoker – only he smoked Camels without filters, and often had a scotch and water in his other hand to accompany the cigarette.

Howard's mother, Bess, is of Greek descent. She was always busy. If she wasn't at the dental office, she was in the kitchen cooking up a Greek feast, or down in the basement ironing bed linens or the men's underwear and t-shirts.

Howard's brother, John, was 12 years old and played in a rock and roll band. His sister, Connie, was married to Allen, a 2nd lieutenant in the Air Force. They were stationed in San Bernardino, California.

Peppy, their poodle, was a fond member of the family also. He would often sneak up when no one was looking and get the butter out of the butter dish on the dining room table. Benny, the cockatiel, had a fancy bird cage in the kitchen and was chirping constantly.

On Sunday afternoons Howard would often take me boating at Lake Geneva, Wisconsin. We'd pick up a six pack of beer, rent a boat and speed around the lake all afternoon. He liked nothing better than driving the boat as fast as he could, making sharp turns, and listening to me squeal with delight. On several occasions, he sheared the pin on the boat and we had to be towed back to the rental facility.

Howard's grandpa, the first Howard E. Querry, lived on a cranberry marsh in Wisconsin. His second wife, Jane, was 20 years younger. Howard took me there once to meet them. Jane catered to her husband, Howard, hand and foot, just like Bess did with her Howard, at home and in the dental office.

Grandpa had the same dry sense of humor as his son and grandson, yet was much taller and very distinguished-looking, even in the flannel shirt he often wore. I remember him sitting in his rocking chair by the fireplace in his secluded Wisconsin home.

In the beginning of the summer, I was dating another man, Bob, a bank auditor, who was older – 27. As the summer progressed, I spent more and more time with Howard and less with Bob.

At the end of that glorious summer, I told the bank, Bob and Howard I was going back to Carbondale to finish my second year of college. I was enrolled in a two-year vocational training program to be a legal secretary. Howard was disappointed and tried every trick he could come up with to get me to stay in the Chicago area, but I was committed to my education.

Not long after I left Chicago, Bob came to visit me in Carbondale. We went for a walk in the woods on a beautiful Fall day and he asked me to go steady with him and stop dating Howard. I couldn't. After Bob returned to Chicago, he sent me a touching goodbye letter quoting Kahlil Gibran speaking all about love:

> *When love beckons to you, follow him,*
> *Though his ways are hard and steep.*
> *And when his wings enfold you yield to him,*
> *Though the sword hidden among his pinions may wound you.*
> *And when he speaks to you believe in him,*
> *Though his voice may shatter your dreams as the north wind lays*
> *waste the garden.*

I cried when I read his letter. As hard as it was to stop seeing him, I had to; my feelings for Howard were stronger.

Shortly after that weekend with Bob, Howard called to tell me he had quit his job at the Bank of Oak Brook and was enrolled for the next semester at St. Louis University, which was about two hours from Carbondale. Both of his uncles were graduates of St. Louis University. I think they pulled some strings and got him enrolled quickly. He wanted to enroll in college to avoid the draft.

So despite my best intentions to the contrary, I let myself fall in love with the skinny man I met in Chicago during the summer of '65. I'm a pretty tough nut to crack, I've been told, but Howard did it. My heart opened up and let him in.

We started spending every weekend together. He'd either come to Carbondale and stay with some friends of mine, or he'd come and pick me up and take me to St. Louis for the weekend. He'd rent a room for me in the girl's dorm. We'd laugh all weekend and drive around in his Ford Fairlane with the top down – my long blonde hair blowing in the wind, and me sitting as close as I could get to him.

Our good times ended all too abruptly, however. Because he didn't maintain a high enough grade point average, he got kicked out of St. Louis University. He wasn't interested in studying but more in living life to the fullest. So he moved to Carbondale and got a job as a retail clerk in a grocery store.

Early in August of '66, the letter that would alter our lives forever came in the mail – his draft induction notice. Even though we were expecting it, when it came a dark cloud descended upon our joy-filled lives. The Army and the war in Vietnam were the only things that could separate us, and they were about to.

A few weeks later I took him to the station in Carbondale, where he boarded a train headed for the army induction center in St. Louis. From there he went to Fort Leonard Wood for basic train-ing. It wasn't the same in Carbondale without his broad smile and light-hearted ways.

I graduated with my associate degree as a legal secretary and moved back to Prairie du Rocher to live with my parents. Within a week or so I got a job working for a lawyer in St. Louis, an hour commute from my parents' home.

On October 2nd, my 21st birthday, I went to visit Howard at Fort Leonard Wood. He managed to get a couple of hours off. We laughed all afternoon. He marched the men in his platoon out to sing "Happy Birthday" to me. He always made me laugh, no matter how many things we had to be sad about. On the two audio tapes he sent from Vietnam, he was still laughing and joking. He was good for me in that respect. I tend to take things much too seriously.

It was hard to leave him that day at Fort Leonard Wood. They had shaved his head – he looked like a prisoner of war. I began to get a sense of what the Army was doing to my boyfriend – stripping him of his tenderness. It made me sad. I hated the Army for what they had done to his hair and for taking him away from me.

After basic training, he was sent to Ford Ord, California for Advanced Infantry Training. He was told that after that eight week program, he'd be sent to Vietnam.

In a letter I wrote to his parents at the time I expressed the following sentiments:

> *I'm not going to worry because I am confident*
> *my prayers will bring him safely back to us.*

I'm not sure if that was blind faith or denial, perhaps a little bit of both. I was trying desperately to keep everybody's spirits up – Howard's, his parents', my parents', and my own.

During his Advanced Infantry Training at Ford Ord he applied for and was accepted into Officer Candidate School at Fort Benning, Georgia, thus postponing his tour of duty in Vietnam a little longer.

When Howard and I got engaged in April of '66, he wanted to get married immediately. I told him I didn't want to take any chances of finding a job on an Army base. I convinced him that I needed to keep my job in St. Louis as a legal secretary. I suggested we get married when he returned from Vietnam. He didn't want to wait that long.

With the marriage issue unresolved, he went off to Fort Benning for Officer Candidate School and I went to work every day, stashing away every penny I could, so we wouldn't be so financially strapped when we did get married. We saw each other infrequently during this time, but talked on the phone every weekend, and I wrote him every day. He was a determined young man – determined to become an officer and determined to marry me.

After twelve weeks of Officer Candidate School, he called me one evening sounding so depressed, I knew something was terribly wrong.

Grief Denied

"What's the matter, Howie?"

"Honey, I got dismissed from OCS today. They told me I lacked organization and was indecisive. Will you still marry me?"

"Let's talk about it when we see each other," I responded.

He invited me to come to Fort Benning for a formal dinner and dance celebrating the completion of the first twelve weeks of OCS. I bought a new dress, a pair of dyed linen shoes to match, grabbed my short white gloves and a strand of pearls and jumped on a plane headed for Fort Benning. I couldn't get there fast enough.

At the end of the evening he borrowed a car and drove down a winding country road. When he parked the car we hopped out. He took me by the hand and led me over to a high knoll where we could see the brilliant star-studded sky. He pointed to the brightest star in the heavens,

"See that star?"

I nodded.

"I'm going to put that star in your pocket. Will you marry me soon?"

He promised me the brightest star in the heavens. How could I refuse?

"Yes, I'll marry you soon."

That night we slept together for the first time, but we didn't make love. We wanted to but instead we held each other all night dreaming about the day when we'd have that bright shiny star in our pocket.

After being dismissed from Officer Candidate School, Howard was then sent to the NCOC Academy to train to be a sergeant. Because of the high casualty rate of sergeants in Vietnam, they needed replacements and the NCOC Academy was established to fill the gap. Howard was in the first graduating class.

After that weekend in Georgia, I returned to my parents' home and reality set in. I wondered how we'd ever make it on the salary of an enlisted man and I also wondered how I'd survive the year he had to spend in Vietnam. I always worried about the circumstances of our lives and Howard worried about when we'd see each other again.

The irony of being kicked out of OCS for lacking organization and not being decisive enough, and then being sent to the NCOC Academy to train to become an infantry sergeant was baffling to me. If he wasn't decisive enough to be an infantry officer, how could he be decisive enough to be a squad leader?

Putting all that aside, I started planning the big wedding I'd always dreamed about. I informed my boss I'd soon be leaving to begin my life as an Army wife.

Howard managed to get a few days off during his rigorous training schedule to come home and get married. My mother and I had everything ready when he flew home that Thursday evening. I drove to the airport in St. Louis that night all by myself. I wanted some time alone with him before our wedding day.

Waiting eagerly at the gate as everyone piled off the plane, I thought he'd be the first one off to greet me with open arms. I waited and waited – he didn't come. Pretty soon, the people stopped coming and there was no Howard. Did the Army change its mind about letting him have the time off? Where was he? I asked the flight attendant to check and see if there was anyone on the plane. Ten minutes later she came out with Howard. He had fallen asleep and didn't even wake up when the plane landed. He stumbled into the airport lobby rubbing his eyes and joking about it all as usual.

I was really hurt. How could he fall asleep when he was coming home to marry me? I felt so disappointed that he didn't rush off the plane, twirl me around in circles and tell me how happy he was that I was marrying him. I didn't know at the time what a rigorous training program he was in. The Army was taking away more and more of the young man I had met and fallen in love with.

We were married on Saturday, September 27, 1967, at St. Joseph's Catholic Church in Prairie du Rocher. I insisted that my father rent a tuxedo. I'd never seen him in one. Weakened by diabetes and two eye surgeries for detached retinas, he was very cautious as he walked me down the aisle.

Howard stood at the end of the aisle with a big grin on his face. He had a hint of mischief in his eyes, which I couldn't wait to find out about. His hair had grown out a little so he didn't look quite so much like a prisoner of war.

At the end of our wedding day, we packed our gifts into a small U-Haul, told our families goodbye and headed for Fort Benning. Howard had to be back in time for duty Sunday evening. We had sold his white Ford convertible and bought a brand new, navy blue Chevy II Nova sedan. Princess, our black German Shepherd, was in the back seat.

We drove all the way from southern Illinois to Alabama before we stopped for the night. At 2 a.m. I was exhausted, but quite excited about consummating our love.

Back in '67 some girls were still virgins when they got married. I was. I was certainly interested in sex and had a few opportunities, but couldn't take the risk of killing my mother. When I was a teenager, mom had threatened me, "If you ever get pregnant before you're married, I'll kill myself." I took her threat to heart and kept my virginity intact, saving it all for my husband. As it turned out, he didn't appreciate it very much.

Our first lovemaking was disappointing; it hurt. He wasn't very loving or passionate. I think he was worried about getting back to the base on time. He just rushed through it.

I remember thinking, "Is this what I've been waiting for all these years?"

Grief Denied

There was a big spot of blood on the bed. I didn't know what had happened. I thought he must have ripped something inside me. My mother didn't teach me anything about sex and none of my girlfriends had told me about the hymen breaking the first time you make love.

It wasn't until years later that I discovered why there was blood in the bed that night. If Howard knew, he didn't say anything. I think he had previous sexual experience but I don't know for sure. There was so much we didn't talk about.

We were up and on the road again by 6 a.m. When we arrived at Fort Benning a few minutes late, the Army made Howard stay on base during the entire first week of our marriage as punishment. Thus began my initiation into being an Army wife.

After a week, he came home and we started getting acquainted as husband and wife. Our lovemaking improved. However, Howard always seemed preoccupied during those early months of marriage. I found out years later from Bill Jones what the Army was telling him about Vietnam. He held it all inside and just tossed and turned and tumbled all night when he was supposed to be sleeping.

When he graduated from the NCOC Academy, his parents came for the ceremony. I remember thinking as each candidate walked across the stage to receive his certificate and his orders for Vietnam, that they might as well be handing him a death certificate.

After a 30-day leave, Howard had to report for duty to Fort Ord, California, from where he would ship out to Vietnam. We packed up all our belongings and sent them to my mom's home in southern Illinois. We went to Florida first so Howard could say goodbye to his grandmas, Alma and Marie. Marie gave him a Sacred Heart Scapula to keep him safe in Vietnam. He tucked it into his wallet, and it was still there when his personal effects came back after his death.

After a few days in Florida, we went to the Chicago area to say farewell to his parents. It was heartbreaking. Both Howard and his father were joking right up to the end. They always managed to bring humor to the saddest of events.

Last of all we traveled to my parents' home in southern Illinois where I would be staying when Howard went to Vietnam. Time seemed to go so fast. I guess because we spent it visiting relatives and driving all the way across the country.

Howard and I were afraid to be alone together – to face what was before us. We each carried our own fears but we didn't confide in one another. We couldn't muster up the courage to talk about the possibility of his death.

All the hoping and praying that he'd somehow escape the war didn't work. The threat of Vietnam didn't go away but loomed larger and larger. Eventually it became a reality. He was going to Vietnam and I would have our baby – alone. We planned to meet in Hawaii on his first R&R and I was to bring the baby with me so he could see it. We decided on names for the baby – Michelle for a girl, Howard IV, if it was a boy.

Grief Denied

I'd never seen him look sadder than he did on the day he left, March 8, 1968. His normal high-spirited humor was gone. We didn't even make love on our last night together. Even though he was still with me physically those last few days, his spirit was gone. I think he was already fighting the war, or perhaps worrying about it. Or perhaps he just couldn't face a goodbye if he felt it would be the last one. I kept trying to reach him but was unsuccessful. It was as if he was preparing me to live without him.

It was at least a month before I received my first letter from him.

"Vietnam is unbelievably dirty and hot. There is so much dust around you can't hardly breathe. All you see in the sky are military planes, jets and helicopters. At night mortars are going off all around constantly. It's a good thing I'm a sound sleeper or I'd probably crack up."

In his third letter,

"Tell everyone I'm fine and not to worry, especially you."

He was sent to Bearcat, the home of the Old Reliable, the 9th Infantry Division. Even though I wrote every day, he was there three weeks before he received any of my letters.

In another letter, he wrote:

"I'm a little nervous today. I guess this place is starting to get to me. Sometimes, I get so lonesome for you that I can't hardly stand it. There is never anything to look forward to here except mail call and it's really depressing when you don't get any.

"I'm with my unit now and I'm a squad leader. We're at an old French fort, Fort Courage. It's on the South China Sea. It's on a little island so we're safe as long as we are here. Whenever we go out on a mission we go by chopper and return by chopper. Most of the men in my company get out of the field after six months. Maybe I'll be one of the lucky ones."

His letters were fairly cheerful and after a month there, he said, "So far I've only been in the field three times. Believe me, I'm glad about that. Boy Honey, I'll sure be glad when this year is over so we can be together for the rest of our lives."

He always signed his letters the same:

"I have to go darling. Remember I love you with all my heart and soul. Take care of yourself, the baby and the dog. Okay?

"I sure wish I could feel the baby kicking around inside you. Does it kick all the time? Maybe the baby is nervous like me, do you think so?"

And in one of the last letters I received:

"All the prayers must be doing some good because our whole company has been very lucky so far – somebody must be looking out for us."

In his letter dated April 17, he said they were going to leave the French Fort. He was pretty discouraged because they had done so much to waterproof the place for the monsoons which were about to begin. But they were ordered to leave and go elsewhere. I thought it sounded just like the Army.

When his wallet was returned with his personal effects, it was soaked with water. I remembered he had written, *"I carry my wallet with me and look at your picture wherever I go."*

In one letter he reported an injury sustained by one of his men.

"We were out on an operation yesterday and I lost one of my men, however, it was only a leg wound, so he'll probably be back with us in two or three weeks. When we got back to base camp, we celebrated for two reasons: One – because it was his second purple heart and he'll get off the line, and two – because one of the Gooks in the village is getting married tomorrow. Everybody is hoping we don't go out tomorrow so we can see the wedding. Everybody in the platoon is sick about it because she happens to be the prettiest girl in the village but she doesn't even compare to you. Sometimes I really get a big kick out of being over here, but darling, I miss you so much.

"Sgt. Jackson, our platoon sergeant, saw a rat this morning, grabbed my pistol and shot it, so now we have two kills. The lieutenant fired at one yesterday but he missed. We caught a pigeon in the CP tonight. He came in and pooped on the lieutenant's chest while he was sleeping so we had to capture him. He was going to keep it 'til morning so he'd have plenty of time to think up some devious torture. I told him we should sell it to the Gooks because they'd eat him, so that's what we did. It was really funny.

"Don't worry about me over here. I'm so skinny they can't hit me even if they're shooting at me. I have faith, so don't worry.

"A couple of rats came out and ran around in here today during daylight. That was too much so I pulled out my trusty 38 and shot one of them. The other one didn't come back. Vietnam is nothing but mud, water, rats and mosquitoes.

"It'll be so neat to be together forever without having Vietnam to worry about. We sure are going through a lot together, aren't we Honey?"

And in the next letter,

"Oh, that wedding I mentioned never took place because about three hours before the ceremony, he was called out on an operation. He is in the Vietnamese Army. They were both in tears. War is really a neat thing, huh?

"That guy in my squad that was wounded is in Japan now. One of my team leaders got a letter from him. He has a broken leg so it will probably be at least two months before he's back."

And in his last letter dated May 1st,

"Honey, it's so neat to hear you talk about the baby and how it feels when it kicks. It makes me feel like I'm there with you."

He sent me a letter my brother, Stan, had written to him. At the end my brother had said:

"Take good care of yourself and keep lucking. We all think about you if that helps, I don't know what else we can do."

Every night on the news, I'd see the fighting and the killing of the war. I stopped watching – it brought the reality of the war too close to home for me.

Even though it was nearly impossible for a pregnant woman to get employment in those days, I was fortunate to find a temporary job at Scott Air Force Base in Belleville. It was about 45 miles from where I was living with my parents. I maintained an optimistic attitude, found a good doctor and prayed to God daily to protect Howard.

When I wasn't working, I was fixing up the baby's room. The bedroom which had been my brothers' contained a big double bed and one twin bed. I took out the twin bed, borrowed a bassinet from Howard's Aunt Jane, painted the room blue, got white lace curtains, and put down a new linoleum floor. It looked beautiful, clean and ready for our new baby. On the wall at the end of the bassinet, I hung a map of Vietnam.

My job at Scott Air Force base was boring, but at least it got me out of the house every day. When I wrote Howie I told him about every little move I felt the baby make, how I was fixing up the baby's room, how much I missed him, and how worried I was about getting through the year without him.

In his letters, he'd talk about his R&R and our plans to meet in Hawaii. He was concerned about how much weight I was gaining and asked about it in every letter. I thought it surprising that he didn't have concerns more pressing than my weight. I guess he was worried that I'd gain too much and not lose it after the baby was born.

We both just kept creating our future, even when the going got the roughest, which it soon did.

He was only there two short months before he was killed. From the time I read the article in the paper about his unit being in a battle until they notified me of his death on May 15, I wrote to him every day telling him how terrified I was and how it was affecting me. I was having hard contractions and sleepless nights – afraid to tell my mom for fear she'd make me go to the doctor. My daughter, as a 7-month fetus, was living through this trauma with me.

Seeing the article in the paper was a premonition of his death. The minute I saw it I went into shock. I kept writing letters in a feeble attempt to keep him alive – to absolutely disregard the reality of his death.

On May 10, the day he died, I wrote to him that the peace talks had begun in Paris. On May 12, I wrote telling him that even though we had a house full of guests, I had spent two hours crying in my room because I was so worried. On May 13, I wrote that the fighting had ended in Saigon. I was relieved.

On the morning of May 15, I wrote my last letter to him. That evening they came to inform me of his death. It took the Army five days to find me. After several days of unsuccessful attempts to locate me at Fort Jackson, South Carolina, they contacted Howard's parents who gave them my address and phone number. Didn't Howard tell the Army where I was living? Didn't he fill out a form saying he wanted me to be notified first in the event of injury or death? Doesn't the Army know how to keep simple records?

The Army had terrorized him during his training, sent him away to a war in a foreign land, and now killed him. I developed a deep hatred for and desire for revenge on the Army, my government and my country.

I don't know how I survived the days immediately following the notification of his death. Everyone kept telling me to be strong – I had a life growing inside me and I needed to eat and sleep for the sake of the baby.

I went through the motions of living, but every morning when the sun came up and the realization of his death would hit me, I'd sink into despair again. Sleep was the only reprieve I had. In slumber, I could dream it wasn't true. Every morning, I'd look out of my bedroom window at the big green leaves on the sycamore and realize it was true, he was dead and his body would be home soon. I had to plan a funeral, get a black maternity dress, make the arrangements and above all else, I had to hold back the tears. I had to be strong, everyone kept telling me to be strong.

Every day when reality set in, I'd freeze up a little more, freeze my feelings so I could get through another day – stiffen my body and my baby. I got through those days waiting for his body to arrive from Vietnam, waiting for the phone call from the mortician who was going to pick up his remains at the St. Louis airport; I got through it all by becoming a numb, frozen woman.

When his remains finally arrived at the St. Louis airport on May 23rd, the same airport from which he had departed a few months earlier, the funeral director called to say he was picking up the coffin and it would be ready for viewing the next day.

I drove to the funeral home the following day thinking I would see Howard's dead body clothed in his army uniform, lying neatly in the coffin. The first person I met was the escort who accompanied Howard's body. He was dressed in his Army uniform, wore a black arm band and a pair of white gloves. I don't even remember speaking to him. I blamed him for Howard's death. He was part of the institution that killed Howard – The United States Army.

When the funeral director told us Howard's body was "Non-viewable," my mother-in-law shrieked. Coming from such a quiet reserved woman, the shriek sent chills up and down my spine. I hushed up a little bit more, froze my feelings a little bit more. I couldn't lose it if she was losing it. Somebody had to remain in charge. It was me. I didn't rage, scream or vomit as I felt like doing. I just got quieter and quieter, disappearing a little more every day. I heard someone say his body was in three different pieces or maybe it was wrapped in three different wraps. I can't remember which. My memories are very fuzzy and blurry about that day at the funeral home.

Grief Denied

The funeral director said he had opened the coffin but the smell was so strong he couldn't proceed any further. He said it was better that we not view the body. My brother, Stan, offered to view Howard's body if I wanted him to. He'd been in the Marine Corps and perhaps thought it was his duty to do such dirty work. I didn't insist upon it.

I tried to get through the funeral as peacefully as possible, so I could go to my room and be alone for the rest of my life. I just wanted to be alone. I didn't want to be seen in public. I felt enormous shame that such a terrible thing had happened to me and my husband.

At the cemetery when they fired the 21-gun salute, played taps and handed me the neatly-folded flag from his coffin, I pressed it to my heart, bowed my head and didn't shed a tear. Gus, Howard's uncle, was sobbing out loud.

Betrayed by the God I prayed to daily, I remember wondering if I'd ever understand why this happened. Silly question, I think now. Death isn't understandable, especially death in such a confusing war.

The only thing that kept me going during that time was the life I had growing inside of me. I couldn't give up. I was the instrument through which his child would be born, and I had to continue for the sake of our child.

"It's terrible to wake up in the morning and not want to live but that's the way I feel most of the time. But when the baby starts kicking, I realize I have a very good reason to live… I just can't bear the thought of never seeing him again. I try not to think about it and sometimes I pretend he's coming back."*

I didn't have a name for it then, but denial was pretending that he'd come back someday. My love affair with denial continued for many years. But pretending didn't make my grief go away – it just buried it deeper and deeper.

*Excerpt from a letter written
to his parents after the funeral.

2. Michelle's Arrival

oward would be standing by my bed trying to wake me. When I woke up, he'd be gone.

He would show up at my door and tell me that he had not died in Vietnam, but had been living in Europe with another woman.

I don't remember when these nightmares began. I just remember not being able to fall asleep again after I had one.

After Howard's funeral I began serving my life sentence as a war widow – a solemn, stoic woman. I modeled my behavior after Jackie Kennedy – maintaining a stiff upper lip and a stance of enormous strength. Howard's death was a reflection of my own unworthiness. Poor Howard had hooked up with me, a bad luck charm.

My doctor suggested I go back to work so I did, just a few weeks after the funeral. A military base was probably not the best place to work at the time, but I had no idea what to do with myself. I just did what people told me to do, "Stop crying, be strong and go back to work."

The shame of my father's alcoholism, which I carried throughout my childhood, was now compounded by the shame of having my husband die in this unpopular war.

Grief Denied

I worked right up until a week before our daughter was born. On the evening that my labor started, Mom was out mowing the lawn. When my contractions appeared to be regular, I started timing them. When they remained consistent for an hour, I knew it was time to go to the hospital so I took a shower, put on a clean dress and got my things together to take with me.

When Mom came in, she asked, "Where are you going?

"To the hospital," I said.

She insisted on driving. So we started our 45-mile journey to St. Elizabeth's Hospital in Belleville. After about 20 minutes I asked Mom to pull over and let me drive – I was getting car sick.

Even though this was my first child, I felt fairly calm and certain that everything would be fine. Before Howard left for Vietnam, he went with me on my first visit with my obstetrician, Dr. Burpo.

When I arrived at the hospital, I called my doctor to inform him of my progress. He had used deep-relaxation audio tapes with me in preparation for delivery. Mom put one of the tapes on and I tried to relax as I had done so many times during my pregnancy, but the pains grew increasingly intense.

The pain of childbirth is pain like I'd never felt before or since. It felt as if my back was going to break right in half. Dr. Burpo didn't like to use pain medication so I just screamed when the pains became unbearable. He told me I could. I'm grateful for the good doctor I had. He believed in natural childbirth.

When I was taken into the delivery room, the momentum picked up. The labor pains intensified and I continued to scream, bear down, and P-U-S-H as the doctor and nurses kept telling me to do.

Right before Michelle was born, the doctor positioned a mirror so I could witness the miracle. He did the episiotomy and blood was everywhere. Shortly after that, her perfect little almond-shaped head appeared in the mirror and within moments she was lying on my stomach.

"It's a girl," he said, as he cut the cord and handed her to me.

"Let her nurse," one of the nurses said, so I placed her at my breast and she began sucking.

In that moment, I was in the presence of a miracle – here was a precious baby girl lying in my arms, sucking at my breast. I felt a deep sense of wholeness and profound joy. She looked exactly like Howard and I felt as if I had given birth to him. It was odd. I named her Michelle, the name Howard and I had picked for our baby girl.

After Howard died, we had all hoped for a boy – someone to replace him. But I was thrilled it was a girl. I knew we'd be close.

She was healthy with no apparent defects – ten little fingers and toes. I was relieved. I was concerned about how her father's death had affected her. Because she looked normal I assumed she had survived the trauma without damage, but psychological damage can't be detected by looking at our outsides.

Grief Denied

A few weeks before Michelle's birth I had written to Howard's parents telling them how the baby was going to fill the hole in my heart that Howard's dying had created. And that's exactly what happened. I took all my love and affection for Howard and gave it to my new baby girl. That seems normal and natural and even innocent enough, but years later I struggled with sorting out those misplaced feelings. The love you have for your husband is very different from the love you have for your child. I got the two confused and it affected Michelle in ways I'm still discovering.

Dr. Burpo prided himself on the fact that all his patients walked away from the delivery table. So within an hour of delivery, I walked into the waiting room to tell my faithful mom, who had been listening to me scream through it all, that I had a girl. The nurse followed me carrying the little bundle tightly wrapped in pink blankets.

In the hospital when all the fathers came to see their new babies, I was heartbroken. I felt like the mother of an illegitimate child – the very thing my mother had threatened me with. The nurses didn't know me personally and perhaps didn't know why there was no father coming to visit. I didn't tell them. Perhaps my doctor did, I don't know. No one mentioned the baby's father and I didn't volunteer any information.

There's a certain silence which surrounds death. It's quite uncomfortable for the survivors. No one knows what to say to comfort the bereaved so they often say nothing.

My doctor kept me in the hospital for a week after the delivery. He wanted to be certain everything was back to normal. Mom came to see us every day.

My homecoming from the hospital was sweet. As I stepped onto the cement slab porch and approached the back door to my parents' home, I saw the sign, "Welcome Home, Pauline and Michelle." It was written on butcher block paper from my mother's meat market and attached to the white shingles of the house. It was beautiful. I smiled and posed while my mother took our picture. I carried my seven-pound baby girl into my childhood home, into the room which had been my brothers' bedroom. It was 100 degrees, 100% humidity. I felt shaky. I wondered how Michelle would survive since my parents didn't have an air conditioner.

Here I was with a child, a precious little being that came from inside me a few days earlier. I was bringing her to my parents' home because I didn't have the home her father and I were going to create. Her bassinet was covered with a beautiful lace cover. When I placed her in it, I felt as if I was laying her down in paradise. The map of Vietnam was still there at the foot of her bassinet. I'd tell her about her father when she was old enough to understand.

Princess, curious about this bundle I was bringing into our room, was sniffing her. I assured her that this bundle belonged in this room with us.

Elmer, my father, was anxious to see my baby girl. When she grabbed his big, rough, patchy forefinger, he smiled proudly. He shook his head displaying the sadness he felt about Howard's death. At the same time as he shook his head, he made this distinct sound, "Tsk. Tsk. Tsk." by clicking his tongue on the roof of his mouth.

"Why, oh why has this happened? Why has the good Lord taken this baby's father away? Why didn't he take me instead? I have nothing to live for."

His remarks saddened me. He was bartering with God to see if he could trade his life for Howard's, but it was too late to barter. Howard was dead and buried. As my father mourned the death of my husband, he would cry, shake his head in sorrow and utter, "Tsk. Tsk. Tsk. Tsk."

Elmer would come to Michelle's room several times a day to check on her, to see if she was real, if she was still there. Each morning when he awakened and the last thing before bed at night, he'd venture in. He never kissed her. He just touched her cheek and let her grab his forefinger. As she grew older, she began to recognize him and smile at him.

My daughter enriched my father's life immensely. He had something new and exciting to look forward to everyday – his visits to see his granddaughter. Such a simple thing, but it gave him so much joy. His life was so empty. His retail store was closed. His alcoholism, diabetes and two eye surgeries for detached retina had left him unable to work. So he was on disability.

Nevertheless, he would walk across the street every day, and enter his empty shell of a store and listen to KMOX, his favorite radio station. He sat in that store, Elmer A. Laurent & Sons, eight hours a day with no merchandise to sell, no customers coming in, no life in the building except his own. He smoked cigars, chewed tobacco, stared into space and listened to KMOX. He was pretending, pretending he still had a business.

This baby girl was not pretend, however. Every time he went to check on her, sure enough she was there. He rubbed his rough fingers against her precious soft cheek and talked baby talk to her. The only times I ever saw my father smile were when he was with my baby.

If my father had any love for me, he couldn't express it. He could express his love for my baby, however. I guess it's easier for a father to love a tiny baby girl than to hug and hold his grown daughter whose breasts are overflowing with milk. He never hugged, held or comforted me as a child and even when I had lost my husband, he couldn't offer love, support or comfort. He expected me to comfort him and ease his pain over losing his son-in-law in such a tragic war.

On all the family photographs of my childhood, my sister is sitting on my father's lap. He used to tell me that she was so much prettier than I was. She had dark hair and dark skin as compared to my fair skin, blue eyes and blonde hair. Maybe my father favored my sister because she looked like him or perhaps it was because she was born with a handicap. She is deaf.

Grief Denied

When I married Howard I thought I had overcome my father's rejection of me. But with Howard's death, betrayal continued. I concluded that I just wasn't worthy of getting or keeping a man's love. I assumed that my marriage was a mistake, that God had punished me and that I'd never marry again because I wasn't supposed to be married in the first place.

My mother was a little more emotionally available to me than my father, but not much. She was consumed by her rage about my father's drinking and she spent most of her energy trying to punish him for it. She was sure he could stop if he would just set his mind to it or if he loved her and the children enough.

My three older brothers each played their roles in the alcoholic family. My oldest brother became the hero, the surrogate spouse for my mother. My second brother carried my mother's rage, so he was always in trouble. When my youngest brother, the third son, was born, Mom instructed her sisters, who were her midwives, to throw him in the pig pen. She obviously wasn't too thrilled that she had another boy. This brother became the invisible son in the family. My sister, the first daughter, was my father's favorite. And I was the last child – the lost child – unwanted – a mistake.

My mother practiced the only form of birth control approved by the Catholic church – rhythm. It consists of charting your menstrual cycle on a calendar and abstaining during your fertile days. My mom conceived me only three months after my sister was born. She confessed to me once that she tried to abort me by sleeping on Sears catalogues.

In those days help was not as readily available for families of alcoholics as it is now. I no longer blame my parents for my childhood. Coming to an understanding of the dynamics of my alcoholic family and how it affected me has helped me to develop forgiveness and compassion.

Two weeks after I brought Michelle home from the hospital, she was baptized at St. Joseph's Catholic Church. Howard's sister, Connie, and my brother, Stan, were her godparents.

Howard's parents and his aunts and uncles all came to the baptism to meet his new daughter. I rented St. Joseph's Church Hall to accommodate the guests. Michelle slept soundly all day, seemingly oblivious to everyone who was there to meet her for the first time. People kept trying to wake her to get a glimpse of her eyes.

Howard's Aunt Jane and Uncle Gus bought her baptism outfit – a beautiful long white eyelet dress, with matching jacket, hat, shoes and lace rubber pants. She looked like a little angel.

She received many gifts that day. It was all pretty overwhelming for me. I could see how special she was to all those relatives who had lost Howard.

Howard's father was rather solemn that day, not his usual jovial self. He was far away in his thoughts, I guess. No one mentioned Howard not being there, it was just too painful to even discuss.

Grief Denied

It was my father who informed me that it was time to stop nursing Michelle, "She's getting a little big for that, don't you think." She was only six months old. Because I didn't have a strong sense of myself and because I was longing for my father's love and approval, I let his words influence me. His one comment of disapproval went straight to my heart and I stopped nursing my baby.

The birth of my daughter was my salvation – the relationship I would hide in for years. The circumstances surrounding her birth somehow gave me license to make motherhood the main focus of my life. Michelle gave my life, made empty by Howard's death, meaning and significance. First and foremost I was her guardian – everything else was always secondary.

3. Michelle's Childhood

Michelle was a happy baby. As she grew and developed I photographed every move she made, and entered every peep she uttered in her baby book. Howard's parents were still living in northern Illinois, so we visited them frequently. Mom and I drove to Florida when Michelle was only a few months old so she could meet her two great-grandmothers, Alma Blane and Marie Sotiropoulos, Howard's paternal and maternal grandmothers.

For the first eighteen months of Michelle's life I continued living with my parents and devoted myself entirely to motherhood. I received a pension from the Veterans Administration and my living expenses were minimal, so I didn't have to work. I enjoyed being a mother and was content with watching Michelle grow.

My mother had imbued me with so much shame about having a baby outside of wedlock, that in those early days of motherhood I felt disgrace about being a woman with a child and no husband. Her intention had been to scare me so that I wouldn't conceive a child before marriage. Everyone in the community knew I was a war widow, but it didn't help to dispel the unworthiness I felt about my circumstances. So I isolated myself.

The growing dissention about the war also added to my confusion and isolation. My husband had died in a war that our nation was losing. This compounded my shame. I stopped watching the evening news because all I saw was continued fighting and unrest about the war. I withdrew from it all by simply devoting myself to motherhood.

Living a very isolated life, my only social connection was with my brothers and their families. They were all married with children and lived close by so Michelle got acquainted with her cousins.

My father took a nap every day after lunch at the same time Michelle napped. I kept the house clean, the yard mowed and had dinner ready when my mom returned from her job as a meat cutter at the local grocery store.

One Friday night, as the first anniversary of Howard's death approached, my mother, Michelle and I went to visit my brother Larry and his family who lived in Waterloo, about 45 miles away. Larry and Lola had five daughters and a busy household.

Mother's Day was approaching and we were going to shop for a Mother's ring for Mom. We invited Dad to come along, but he refused as usual. He didn't like to go out after dark because he couldn't see well.

It must have been about midnight when we arrived back home. I always made a point of checking on Dad when we got home from an evening out. I had long ago become his caretaker.

When I opened the door to his room, I saw that his torso was under the bed and his feet were sticking out. I put Michelle down and came back to investigate. I asked Mom to help me pull Dad out from under the bed. When we got him out, I could see that the left side of his face was drawn up and distorted. He was unconscious and breathing heavily.

"I think he's had a stroke, Mom."

"He's drunk. Close the door and let him sleep it off."

"I don't smell alcohol on his breath, Mom."

I called the ambulance and they took Dad to Red Bud Hospital.

My brother Stan and I were holding his hands when he died on May 11, a day and a half later. He never regained consciousness.

When his breathing became increasingly difficult, the nurses and the nuns came in and scurried around him whispering prayers in his ears as he took his last few breaths. Watching his spirit flow right out of his body, I saw death first hand.

The next day when he was all dressed up in his only suit and tie, I lingered at his coffin silently telling him how sorry I was that he died. I was determined to make sure I knew he was dead. I guess I was attempting to make up for not seeing Howard's dead body. Another significant man in my life, dead, without even a goodbye. My resignation and resentment deepened.

I've never denied my father's death as I did Howard's and I think it's because I witnessed his death and saw his lifeless body. I think it's so important to view a loved one's body when they die.

Grief Denied

So a year after Howard's funeral, I followed yet another coffin down the aisle at St. Joseph's. This time I was carrying Michelle in my arms and her very existence was a great consolation in my ongoing despair over another loss I couldn't understand.

Before my father's death, I had planned to go back to school to pursue a degree in education. I thought becoming a teacher would fit in nicely with being a single parent. After my father's funeral I asked Mom to come and live with me and care for Michelle while I attended classes.

Mom sold the home in which she and Dad had raised their family and quit her job as a meat cutter. I found a small house with a large yard, and Mom, Michelle, Princess and I moved to Carbondale, 60 miles south of Prairie du Rocher.

My first two years of college had been a struggle financially. I had to work part-time and borrow money. It was such a blessing to be able to attend school full-time without having to work. I was receiving benefits under the G.I. Bill.

The house we rented in Carbondale didn't have a fenced yard so I had to tie Princess up. The first weekend we were there, she broke her leash and nearly killed the neighbor's dog. When I found her, she had the little dog in her mouth trying to rip it apart. These neighbors didn't have any children. Their dog was as dear to them as a child.

While we were still living in Prairie du Rocher, Princess had become increasingly difficult to deal with. She had bitten one of my nieces as well as an insurance salesman. I was concerned about being liable for her. When she nearly killed the neighbor's dog, it was the last straw. I took her to the Humane Society and left her in a cage with a note explaining that I was donating her. I didn't know what else to do. I had my hands full with going to school full-time and raising my daughter.

The following Monday morning, I got a call from the Humane Society, telling me she was so ferocious she wouldn't let anyone near her to take her out of the cage.

After talking to the vet, I decided to put her to sleep. It was a difficult decision but I didn't see any alternative. She wouldn't even let the veterinarian near her, so I was the one who had to administer the lethal dose.

I think back now and I wonder if she embodied all the rage I felt yet couldn't express. By killing her, I was perhaps attempting to rid myself of my own anger. It didn't work of course. Princess went mad. I did too. It just took me a few more years.

Another part of me died when Princess died. I've always had a strong emotional connection with dogs. As a child, I took great comfort in the pets I had. It seemed easier and safer to trust an animal rather than another human being. Now Princess was gone too. In response, I hardened up and froze my feelings a little bit more.

That spring the students at my university were rioting to end the war in Vietnam. One day on campus I saw a sight that affected me deeply.

Grief Denied

Six men carried a pine coffin across the lawn in front of Morris Library at Southern Illinois University, May 1970.

Where are you going with that coffin? That dead body? That body of my husband. He died there – he didn't know any better, don't punish him, don't hurt him. I'm confused.

These students are mad – they want the war to end and me – where do I fit in? I'm here. I'm a student. I'm part of the protest – the National Guard, the tear gas, the chaos, the pushing, the shoving, the police (pigs they call them).

Look at that man with the fatigue jacket on – he's been to Nam – maybe he knows what he's protesting – maybe he has first-hand experience. I see him around campus a lot. He wears his bronze star and his purple heart on an old floppy, hippie hat. He's making a mockery of my husband's medals. He can't do that. He's intense. He's mad. He's angry. I want to get closer to him, understand his rage, his anger, but I'm scared. I don't know which side to be on. I feel crazy to be in such a turbulent time.

They're threatening to burn the campus. I'm scared. Quiet down, be at peace. I just want to go to school. Be quiet – don't riot, don't burn. Let's talk. Let's have peace. Maybe there's another way. I'm hurt. I'm confused. I want to join with you in protest, but my husband died there. He went there to defend his country. Isn't that why he went? Isn't that why the war is going on? We are fighting communism, aren't we? He died for me and the baby, didn't he? Please don't tell me he died for nothing – no reason, no cause – just another casualty of our government, our political structure, our sickness. Don't tell me it's all for nothing.

I fell in love with the Vietnam veteran who was leading the protest that day. We met at the campus lake one day when I was there alone wearing my red polka-dot bikini. Michelle fell in love with him too. He made me laugh just like Howard used to. One time he came over while I was giving Michelle a bath and got right in the bathtub with her with all his clothes on. She thought that was so funny. She talked about it for years.

Ron was tall, blonde, and handsome – a rebel who was protesting the war, smoking dope, and having sex outside of marriage. He represented a side of life I hadn't yet explored. I'd always been such a good girl following the dictates of my mother, the Catholic church and my country – graciously sending my husband off to be slaughtered in the war in Southeast Asia.

I'd never met a man like Ron. He was ambitious, sexy yet innocent, and very passionate about life and not afraid to show it. He had the courage to protest the war and the killings. I just let my rage sit inside and fester. Good Catholic girls don't protest their government's foreign policy nor disobey their mothers rules about sexuality.

By getting involved with Ron, I was betraying my country and my mother. Being a good girl hadn't paid off, so I became a bad girl. Ron awakened me sexually showing me the depth of passion which can exist between a man and a woman. Howard and I never spent enough time together to develop that. The time we did spend together was so riddled with the threat of Vietnam, neither one of us could relax.

Ron taught me how to smoke dope and encouraged me to join in the war protests. I had a lot of conflict about protesting the war. I couldn't do it. I felt that I'd be betraying Howard. Ron, however, took a very active role in the protests.

Ron and I didn't have any agreements about fidelity. He wasn't interested in being monogamous, and from time to time his yearnings would take him to another woman's bed. He always came back, but each time the split between us deepened.

When we graduated, he with his master's degree and I with my bachelor's, he hinted at marriage, but after living with his mother for a few months, he told me his mom thought he should wait for a virgin – a woman who did not already have a child. Another Catholic mother preaching virginity.

Ron got a teaching job in St. Louis. Mom moved back to Prairie du Rocher and Michelle and I moved to northern Illinois where I got my first teaching job at a private business college.

Ron and I continued to see each other occasionally but I was too much in love with him to be just another woman in his life. So as difficult as it was, I broke off my relationship with him. After Ron, I didn't fall in love again for fifteen years.

When Michelle was 5 years old, I got her a puppy and we spent that summer camping all the way from Chicago to Big Sur, California. Being outside for the whole summer, camping under the stars every night, changed me. Having the freedom to explore and be in close contact with nature created the desire to do more exploration. So when I got back to Chicago, I resigned from my teaching position, packed up a U-Haul, put Michelle and her puppy, Kim, in the back seat and headed west.

I didn't know it at the time, but I was running away – running away from Ron and from all the pain I'd experienced in the state of Illinois. I couldn't outrun the pain however; moving was just another temporary distraction.

Michelle developed a great friendship with her new puppy, Kim, a mixed-breed terrier with short legs and long feathers along her sides. She looked like a golden retriever with short legs. Whenever Michelle and I would have a disagreement, she'd take Kim aside and tell her all her troubles. She slept with Kim every night. Even when she slept on the top bunk of her bed, she wanted Kim up there with her.

On our migration west, Michelle, 5 years old at the time, belted out the lyrics to the John Denver song, *"Rocky Mountain High"* in the back seat of our '72 green and white Dodge Swinger. She learned to blow bubbles on that trip. She was so proud of herself.

We settled in Denver, where I got a teaching job with another business college and Michelle started first grade at Schenck Elementary School.

It was during her early school years that Michelle began to ask questions about her father. When she told her school friends that her dad died in the Vietnam War, she got strange responses. No one else's father had died in a war. She soon learned to be silent about her father because of the response she got from other people. She began to internalize the shame associated with that war.

When Michelle was 7 years old, she asked me, "What would you do, Mommy, if Daddy called you and said he wasn't dead?"

I don't remember how I responded.

When she was in fourth grade, her homeroom teacher, a young man, transferred to another school in the middle of the year. She had a very hard time when that happened. She must have adopted this male teacher as a father figure and when he left, I think she felt abandoned.

When she was 13 years old, she asked about her dad in a more serious way. I had told her that I had a letter which I had written to her when she was 2 years old. She wanted to see it. I dug the letter out of my safe deposit box and gave it to her.

For the first time she cried about her dad. As I held her she said "Maybe the reason my dad died was so that I would be close to you. I would never have been this close to you, if he had lived."

At 13, she was beginning to try to piece together the puzzle of her father's death – why such a tragedy had happened in her life.

At this same time, she began having nightmares about death. She'd come into my bed in the middle of the night terrified from a dream she'd had. I would comfort and reassure her that everything was all right – there was no danger of her death. I didn't know at the time that her nightmares were symptoms of post traumatic stress disorder – a delayed reaction to the trauma of her father's death.

That summer she was scheduled to fly to my mother's for a visit. She was so frightened she insisted I change the reservation to a different day. I changed the flight to another day and she flew, but she was very upset and nervous about it.

Michelle's high school years were marked with increasing distance between us. In search of herself, she ventured from the punk crowd with shaved heads and black clothes to the athletes who went to all the school dances. In her senior year she finally settled in with a crowd where she felt most comfortable.

At the end of her freshman year, she had a straight "A" average. She took herself out of all the advanced classes she was in and put herself in the normal classes so she could be with her best friends. After that first year, I never saw her open a book. She maintained a "B" average without even studying. I tried my best to encourage her to go to college, but she wasn't interested. I blamed Howard since he was never interested in academics either.

At one point during her senior year, I kicked her out of the house. She wasn't abiding by the simple rules I had established and I told her that if she couldn't obey the rules she had to leave. She made one phone call and someone in a Mercedes picked her up in front of the house. I didn't see her for a week. After a few days, I started calling her girlfriends trying to locate her. When I finally reached her, I begged her to come home.

As a graduation gift, I signed us both up for a two-week bike trip to Cape Cod, Martha's Vineyard and Nantucket. At the last minute she decided not to go. She stayed home with her boyfriend instead. I went by myself.

After high school she got a part-time job and when she wasn't working, she was with her friends. I suffered from empty nest syndrome. We'd always been so close – now her friends were more important than me.

When Michelle graduated from high school, I gave her Howard's wedding ring, which we had sized to fit her finger. It's a simple gold band with an diagonal inlay of three small diamonds. She has worn it ever since.

4. My Lost Years

And a ship without rudder may wander
aimlessly among perilous isles
yet sink not to the bottom

The Prophet
Kahlil Gibran

As the years following Howard's death passed, the unresolved loss became increasingly difficult to contain. To dissipate it I continually changed all the outer circumstances of my life – jobs, relationships, and locales. None of those changes ever brought long-lasting relief. They just postponed the explosion of the time bomb inside me. It never occurred to me to begin to look inward for resolution.

Constantly looking and longing for a relationship and an organization where I belonged, I wandered around like a lost child. I was discontented with my life and looking for solutions, as always, when a friend invited me to attend an introductory seminar for the "est" training. Everyone at the seminar that evening had an incredibly high energy. It was contagious. Something about the structure and orderliness of the meeting appealed to me as well.

Werner Erhard, the founder of est (Erhard Seminar Training), was a charismatic man, a used-car salesman from the East Coast who had moved to California, changed his name and begun a whole new life.

His philosophy was that people take responsibility for themselves and get on with their lives. It all sounded ideal to me. I was certainly interested in putting the past behind me and beginning anew.

The training promised transformation in only two weekends. After rushing out and buying the book, *"est - 60 Hours That Transform Your Life"* and consuming it in one evening, I was convinced it was just what I needed. I signed up to do the introductory workshop in April of '77, nine years after Howard's death.

The two weekends left me with the feeling that I was responsible for everything that had happened to me in my life. But I couldn't quite "get it" about being responsible for my husband's death.

I see now that by getting involved in Werner's work, I did just what Howard did when he joined the Army. He surrendered his personal life to defend his country against Communism. I joined Werner's organization to transform the world through the est training. I didn't know it at the time but I was setting out to save the world when I hadn't even saved myself. Joining up with Werner's crusade seemed like a good idea at the time.

After the initial two-weekend training, there were weekly seminars on a number of topics: The Body, Sex, Breakdowns, and The Family. I took all the seminars and all the courses that Werner offered. I couldn't get enough. I had such an increased sense of self-worth when I was at the est center that I volunteered 20-30 hours a week and became a team leader. The assistant's name tag carried a lot of prestige. A staff name tag carried even more. The seminars grew and Werner flourished.

Werner was in the business of transforming lives and I sure loved being a part of it. Working with his organization fulfilled a longing I had for satisfying work. Nothing was sweeter than staying up until 2 or 3 a.m. assisting in one of the trainings, and then hearing the graduates proclaim the wonders of the course the following day.

When I was involved with his organization, I was high on life most of the time. The only problem was that, as is the case with a lot of addictions, I had to keep coming back to get another fix.

In 1985, eight years after I had taken the initial training, I enrolled in the 6-Day Course. It was held on the East and West Coasts only. I chose to do my course at the West coast site in Northern California. It was a rigorous course, both physically and emotionally. There was a one-mile run every morning, a ropes course with three different events, and many hours of sitting in the course room confronting one's "act." Werner believed each of us had an "act" and his job was to expose each person's to them. My "act" was "poor pitiful me." The course guaranteed transformation of one's "act."

My unexpressed grief over losing Howard was buried deeper and deeper during my years with Werner. Werner taught us that the past was the past and it wasn't good to dwell on it, but rather to get on with life. There was a lot of talk about completing the past, but that meant cleaning up any unresolved relationships with people.

For example, we were told Werner had made amends to his ex-wife and children whom he left on the East Coast when he came to California, changed his name and started a new life. They had forgiven him and supposedly were a part of his extended family with his current wife and children who lived on the West Coast. I never heard anything about how to deal with a significant loss that had occurred through death – death in an unpopular war.

One of the insights I gained during the 6-Day Course was into the nature of my affairs with men. I discovered that like a black widow spider who drinks the blood of her prey and then discards them, I was punishing all the men I met for the betrayals of my father, my husband and my Vietnam vet boyfriend. I was sickened to see this but understood that the first step in changing behavior is to become aware of it.

The self which I developed during the years I was involved in Werner's network was not my true self, but more of the false persona I created after Howard died – the pushy broad you wouldn't want to mess with. No one was going to hurt me again. That persona was the protective shell I built around my broken heart. I kept trying to achieve health, happiness, and success, but inside me there was a deep wound continuing to fester. It surfaced every time I slowed down. So I never slowed down.

When I finished the 6-Day Course and left Northern California, I felt as if I was leaving part of myself behind. The people who produced the course were an elite group – the most physically fit of Werner's staff. When I got back to Denver I volunteered even more time at the est center there. A year later I went back to the 6-Day Course to be part of the volunteer team that helped produce the course. Michelle went with me and we had a great time. I felt an even stronger pull to stay at the site.

At the time, I was doing outside sales for a manufacturer of cold-air inflatable advertising balloons. I thought I was successful at my job, so I was quite alarmed when I got laid-off. The lay-off sent me into a downward spiral; it was difficult to find work that was fulfilling.

I began a job search, looking in the newspaper, going on interviews, trying to find exactly what I wanted. One day Michelle suggested that since I spent so much time assisting with Werner's organization I should work for them. I jumped at the idea and began to pursue employment with them.

There happened to be an opening for a finance manager at the 6-Day Course in Northern California. I went through a series of intense, lengthy interviews. I passed them all and was hired.

During the interviews with Werner's management team, I got the feeling that I was going through some sort of renunciation, giving up all my rights – almost like one would do if joining a monastic order or even the military. It became obvious that my personal life was over and I was devoting the rest of my life to Werner, his courses and the work he was doing in the world.

Michelle didn't want to come to California with me so I told her she could get a roommate and continue to live in our home. She was 19 years old and I think, rather lost herself, not knowing what to do after high school. Her teen years had been difficult for both of us.

Leaving her behind in Denver was one of the hardest things I've done in my life. It felt like everything was backwards. Instead of my child leaving home, I, the parent, was leaving. When the U-Haul was all loaded and I was ready to begin my journey, I asked Michelle to come outside and wave goodbye. She couldn't. All she could do was lie on her bed and cry.

I look back now and wonder how I was ever able to leave her. I guess like all the other times in my life, when I've felt a deep instinctive urge to do a particular thing and followed that urge, everything always turned out. Even though this separation was painful for both of us, intuitively I knew it was right. It was inevitable. It was what we both needed for the next phase of our lives to unfold. So this time I made a move all by myself feeling as though I was on a pilgrimage home.

On my journey West I had a lot of time to reflect on my life. I just knew that the move I was making was right both emotionally and vocationally. I was certain that producing Werner's courses on transformation was my chosen path. I had found my niche and moving to Northern California was a dream come true.

My new job was difficult. Not only did I have to learn all the tasks of the finance manager, but I had to learn how to be an employee of Werner Erhard and Associates.

On my first night at the 6-Day Course I was awakened at 2 a.m. by one of the staff members. He informed me that the site was on fire and everyone was being evacuated. Only one house was lost and no one was injured, but later I wondered about that first night and the fire – not a very peaceful homecoming for me.

I cringe when I think of what I subjected myself to during those three months of training. I worked three 12-hour days, followed by two 15- hour days and then had two days off to recover. I don't know how I endured.

The 6-Day Course was located on approximately 350 acres of wooded land in Sonoma County, California. I was assigned to live in a two-bedroom house with another staff member and her boyfriend. I was shocked to find that she smoked cigarettes. I assumed that since the course didn't allow participants to smoke, the staff didn't smoke either.

Some of the staff were sexually promiscuous – not that I was a saint by any means, but I usually held the pretense that I was in love with someone before I slept with them. Because my ideas were different, I was considered an old maid and a prude. I put aside their sexual behavior, thinking perhaps there was something wrong with me because I felt the way I did. I was one of the oldest staff members and maybe I was a prude.

Grief Denied

After three months of grueling training, I was certified as the finance manager and allowed to begin training on the ropes course.

In my front yard were deer, rabbits, and wild flowers. It was paradise. The site was beautiful and I felt a part of something that was powerful and good.

After I was at my new job for only a few months, I got an alarming call from Michelle. Someone had broken into our house, robbed her, and left a threatening note with her name on it. I would have gone back to Denver in a minute, but my manager wouldn't let me. They needed me to help produce the course. I'd have to support her from a distance. So I called her every day on my break to help her get through the incident. When I went back to Denver for a visit three months later, she told me she wanted to move to California.

So she and I loaded up a U-Haul with all her things. We went through everything that we had accumulated while living in our house for ten years – selling or giving away many precious items which we wouldn't have room for in California. We put the house on the market, told all her childhood friends goodbye, put her dog, Kim, in the back seat of her '80 Honda Civic station wagon and headed west.

In Wyoming we encountered a blizzard, and after spending three days stranded in a motel, I called a moving company to come and pick up the contents of the U-Haul. We made a mad dash for California. I couldn't be late. Much like in the military, tardiness was frowned upon in Werner's organization.

The structure and orderliness of Werner's organization provided a rigid container that didn't allow for outbursts of emotions – a safe place where my grief could never slip out. If my physical environment was orderly, then my mental and emotional life would be too.

Many times staff members were sent home to clean their rooms when they were not producing efficiently at work. When Werner was expected on the site, the staff would spend days cleaning toilets with toothbrushes making sure there was not a pubic hair in sight. We always had to keep our homes and our work place impeccable but when Werner came to visit, we really got into an anal retentive mode.

Michelle stayed with me for a couple of weeks until she found a place to live – a studio apartment in the basement of a larger home on the Silverado Trail in Napa Valley. She got a job as a bank teller in Calistoga, a small town much like the one where I lived when Michelle was born. The bank was similar to the one where Howard worked when I met him. Calistoga is only about a 20-minute drive from where I lived and worked at the 6-Day site.

My job was very demanding. I worked approximately 66 hours a week. On my days off, I'd run errands, do the laundry and rest. Michelle came to visit whenever she could. We included her in our family of staff when we had dinners and get-togethers. She fell in love with one of my co-workers, Sy, a Hawaiian. She'd see him on his days off. Since he didn't have a car, she would come and pick him up at the site. He was always singing to her, playing his ukulele, taking her out to the ocean and cooking Hawaiian dinners for her. He was so romantic. She blossomed when she was with him. She looked so beautiful and alive during those years with Sy.

Those of us who worked for Werner knew that our first priority was the company, everything else came second. Michelle wasn't accustomed to being second. She never had been. I think it was difficult for her to have both a boyfriend and a mother with such demanding work schedules.

A year or so after her move to California, she had to put Kim to sleep because she had developed kidney problems and was declining rapidly. Michelle asked me to come over on my lunch hour and go with her to the veterinarian. It was difficult to watch her say goodbye to her companion of 15 years.

She had also just broken up with Sy. Losing him and her dog so close together was heartbreaking. She told me the only way she could sleep was to take a dose of cough syrup that contained codeine.

A couple of weeks later she met Scott Monhoff at a party. Calistoga is such a small town that when somebody new comes to town, everyone notices. Michelle asked the guy who was hosting the party if his friend, Scott, could give her and her girlfriend a ride home. She's very skilled at getting what she wants, just like her father. If there's a way, she finds it.

She and Scott had their first date a couple of days later on July 4, 1989. Scott grew up in Calistoga. He is a building contractor who drives a red pick-up truck, wears Levi's, tank tops and a Raider's baseball cap. He's cute with dark hair, long curly eye lashes and a captivating smile. He's well-built with dark skin and an air of confidence, or perhaps better put, a little bit of cockiness about him. He has the same wild, reckless nature that Howard had. I wonder how Michelle found a man so much like her father when she never even knew him. My friend Charlie says, "She's just like her mom, attracted to that type of guy."

My work with Werner progressed well. After a difficult training period at the tyrol (one of the events on the ropes course), I was transferred to the zipline (another event on the ropes course) and within a month or so, was certified as the bottom director of the zipline.

At the zipline, after being geared up and instructed about safety, participants would walk out to the edge of a plank which was approximately a foot wide and about 200 feet up in the air. They would grab a pair of handlebars and jump off. The purpose of the zipline was to face fear and go beyond it.

When they arrived at the bottom, I was there to unhook them from the lines and welcome them back to earth by giving them a hug. I felt like a midwife assisting at their birth. The men would usually pick me up and swing me around in a circle. Some of the women would just sob and tremble in my arms. I would then turn them around and have them look up at the tiny plank from which they had jumped.

Those days at the zipline were some of my happiest. Even though the work was very demanding, the staff was supportive and committed to each other. I found out how much I could get done in a day when I worked there. I was continually amazed at my own and the other staff members' abilities to take on more and more responsibility and not be overwhelmed by it. It was as if we were super-humans. When we had days off, we'd turn our jobs over to another staff member. They would do their job, plus ours.

My job on Werner's staff was the first one I ever succeeded at. It was also the first time I stayed with a job for nearly three years. I think that was due to the fact that I was part of a team of people committed to a larger purpose. We were hard on each other and expected a lot but we cared in the same way that, perhaps, combat veterans do. We bonded together in the enormity of the tasks before us every week.

I've heard combat veterans speak about the bond between them. They endured the war for each other, not for the body count, nor the territory they would gain, but to stay alive and keep each other alive.

Each week a new team of volunteers came to help us produce the course. They adored us. We were trained to be incredibly capable and competent. It was demanded of us because we all had so much responsibility and if one person didn't carry their share, the whole system broke down.

It was at the 6-Day Course in the Fall of '89 that I fell in love again. Tom was tall, dark and handsome and came to assist on the ropes course nearly every weekend. By some strange coincidence he often ended up at the zipline with me. He was an athlete, a runner. My job didn't allow me to socialize with the volunteers, so I'd only see him on weekends when he came to assist.

Eventually I started seeing him on my days off. I'd tell him about my longing for a man and how I had placed a personal ad in the paper and was beginning to look around. One day he jokingly suggested he and I become lovers rather than me continue to search for someone else. This struck me as rather odd. I'd never before had a friend become a lover. But I was pretty much game for anything.

In Werner's organization if a staff member wanted to become lovers with another staff member or a volunteer, she had to ask permission. It seems bizarre for me to consider this now, but it was part of the rules we all played by. I felt like a young high school girl asking daddy if it was acceptable to sleep with a boyfriend. This rule existed supposedly to prevent the staff from sleeping with the volunteers without any forethought.

The night Tom and I made love for the first time, the whole staff knew about it. The word spread fast. There was little privacy in such an intimate living environment.

Andrew Harvey, a modern day mystic, says,

> *"When two people go to bed together, they have to be awake to the fact that they are now entering no man's land, a place where the darkest powers can disturb them, where they may be exposed to the saddest parts of their psyche."*

Such proved to be the case with Tom and me. We were much better at being friends than at being lovers, and our sexual involvement became the deepest wound we were to inflict upon each other.

Tom came to the special staff dinners and I introduced him as my boyfriend. He was very sweet and kind, had a trim, athletic body, especially muscular legs and was a great lover. We spent my days off together and frequently he stayed with me in the little house where I lived on the site.

I often led the morning exercises for the people in the course. I prided myself on being one of the oldest and most fit staff members of such an elite group. I was in good shape, both physically and emotionally.

That second year on staff, 1989, was one of the happiest of my life. I loved working with people and helping them achieve new levels of joy and satisfaction in their lives. And I loved my new boyfriend, Tom.

I'll never forget the day a man who had been in the course came up to me in the dining hall and asked to speak with me. He said, "The hug you gave me at the bottom of the zipline was the most profound expression of love I've ever experienced in my life."

I felt a wave of heat coming from him that nearly knocked me over. Comments such as this were common in Werner's courses. The course was designed to open people up. As staff members, we were the ones they often stood face-to-face with in those tender moments.

After learning nearly all phases of the 6-Day Course and participating in almost all of them as a leader, I was respected and admired as a senior staff member.

At the end of my second year at the 6-Day Course, a woman who managed one of Werner's offices in a nearby city asked me to come to work for her. I thanked her for asking, but told her I was quite happy where I was. She continued to ask me however, thinking perhaps she could wear down my resistance. I repeatedly refused.

A few days later, I was summoned to the Oak House, the big house where the course leaders stayed when they were on site. One of the course leaders encouraged me to go to work for this woman. I stood firm in my commitment and said,

"No, thank you, I'm happy where I am."

A few days later Werner himself was on the site leading a course and called me in for an interview with him. Walking up to the Oak House to meet with him that day, I could feel my heart pounding in my chest. I was terrified. I'd never had a personal interview with Werner.

I wasn't able to maintain my position with Werner. Within the first few minutes of the interview I told him I'd make the move.

Grief Denied

Years later in a session with my therapist, I understood what actually happened in that interview with Werner. It's called "fusing with the perpetrator" and often occurs when children who have been abused and/or neglected are in the presence of an authority figure. They completely abandon themselves in the face of such an authority.

When I told Werner I would leave the site and take the job, I knew I was making a mistake. I could feel it in my gut. But I did what I had always done in the past – sacrificed myself to meet the needs of somebody else. I found my replacement, trained her and moved off the site into an apartment in the San Francisco Bay area. I asked Tom to come with me.

Tom had trouble finding satisfying work just as I did. He was unemployed at the time. He decided to come with me and look for work in the area I was moving to. What I didn't know when he came with me was that he was leaving a financial mess behind.

After a month of living with me, he found a job as an electronic technician, but got fired within the first couple of weeks. One day I came home earlier than usual and found him at the apartment watching television. He had been fired and hadn't told me. A month later he gave me a check for half the rent and when it bounced, some of my personal checks were returned because of insufficient funds. I was furious. I asked him to move out.

I allowed a man only one mistake and he had made a big one. Things were never the same. I didn't trust him anymore and our relationship disintegrated. We continued to see each other, but I never forgot that betrayal. One thing led to another and I soon found out he was sleeping with other women while professing his true love for me. The door to my heart slammed shut again.

In Werner's network I learned to keep moving and fighting for what I wanted, to not let circumstances get me down, but to continue to plow forward toward my goals. When I left my job at the 6-Day Course I had just been accepted into the Potential Forum Leaders Program, a training program which would train me to lead Werner's courses. I was quite proud to have achieved such a position within the company.

My first orientation meeting for the program was in Washington, D.C. I thought there would be about 200 people at the orientation but there were only about fifteen. I was shocked. Not many people were qualified to be in the program.

When I finished my weekend orientation with Werner's group, I had some free time, so out of curiosity, I took a cab to The Vietnam Veterans Memorial. It was October of '89 and more than twenty-one years after Howard's death.

As I got out of the cab and approached the black granite wall, I felt as if I were entering a tomb – a tomb that contained my dead husband and all my unexpressed grief. A deep foreboding feeling came upon me as I began to walk towards The Wall. It frightened me so much I turned around, hailed a cab and got out of there quick. I obviously wasn't ready for the descent into those feelings.

Grief Denied

I joined the Army when I went to work for Werner. I abandoned my personal life and took on a larger purpose in much the same way that Howard did when he joined the Army and went to Vietnam. And just as being in the Army killed Howard, working for Werner nearly killed me too.

5. The Descent Into Hell

When I made the move Werner asked me to make, the happy life I had at the 6-Day Course dissolved into madness. The position I accepted was one the company had a difficult time filling. I soon learned why. The manager of the office where I went to work managed people by demeaning and diminishing them. I'd been managed by several of Werner's managers, but never by one who was as verbally abusive as she was.

At first I thought that my job was stressful simply because I was new and that it would eventually get better, but from the very start, I heard stories from other staff members of instances where people had resigned without a word of explanation, and how once when someone tried to resign, the manager blocked her at the elevator and wouldn't let her leave.

When I began working with this woman I was very competent – a Potential Forum Leader. At the end of each day I spent with her, I'd lose a couple inches of myself. By the time I resigned, I practically crawled out on my hands and knees.

One day when I was on the phone with a customer, she yelled,

"Don't say that. Put 'em on hold."

When I did, she yelled again instructing me what I should say to them. When I got back on the phone, she started shouting again because I wasn't saying exactly what she had told me to say. The customer on the phone wanted to drop one of our courses and my job was to convince her not to. Werner's managers had to report weekly statistics on the number of people who dropped out of the courses. There was a lot of pressure to have few drop-outs. It didn't matter what the reason was for the person's decision to drop, my job was to keep them in the course.

Another time while I was on the phone with a customer she came over to my desk and starting throwing items from my desk on the floor. At the same time, she was talking to me in a very demeaning manner. I stood up, looked her in the eye and said,

"Stop it."

She retreated and went back to her desk. That was the only time that I ever stood up to her.

Another day during a meeting with the assistants, she began ridiculing me and the other staff members who were present. It was so humiliating. There I was right back in my childhood with my brothers. It was familiar, it was like home.

When I accepted the job at the 6-Day Course, I made an agreement to stay two years. Nothing short of death itself was grounds for "breaking your word" with Werner. When you gave your word to him, it was considered a sacred trust.

When I went to work for this woman, she asked me to sign a contract saying I would stay for three years. After only a few months with her, I couldn't bear the thought of staying three years. It was difficult to break my word, but I did.

My decision to leave came when a good friend who had known me during my two previous years at the 6-Day Course said to me one day, "You've aged about ten years in the few months you've been here."

So I walked away from the job, the organization, and the savior I'd been associated with for thirteen years. That loss precipitated a period in my life when I entered what is often called "the dark night of the soul." I call it "the descent into hell."

Never in my life have I touched such depths of despair as I did during the following year. I'm thankful I survived it. I could easily be just another statistic, my life ended too soon by my own hands.

Michelle described this period in my life like this:

> *"Everyone who knew my mom couldn't believe how much she had changed. All her friends and family were shocked that her outlook on life had become so negative. She had always been so happy and such an outgoing person. She completely changed into a negative, nasty woman."*

I began to suspect something was wrong, when I realized one day that I could smell my own body odor. I looked in the mirror, and didn't recognize the person I saw. It was shocking to see that my lips were so dry they were bleeding. I looked like a woman who was living in the streets. I had a roof over my head, but no spirit left to claim as my own. There wasn't a reason to get up in the morning, to bathe, eat or even to keep myself presentable. I had lost my will to live.

For thirteen years I'd been involved with Werner's organization which taught me to put my feelings aside and to climb the ladder of success by strengthening my self-will. Werner held the position of God in my life for all those years. I thought he had all the answers.

After surrendering to Werner and his organization, just as I had done to Howard, I was betrayed again. Another devastating blow, the loss of a career, a network, and a man I idolized all sent me into confusion and loss of purpose. So I sat and stared into space and let my rambling mind take me on one adventure after another, enticing me to rid myself of despair by committing suicide.

The first step was to get rid of all my possessions so that my daughter wouldn't be burdened with doing it. One weekend, I opened the door to my apartment and started selling everything I owned. Wedding gifts and a homemade quilt made by my dear Aunt Addie were sold for nearly nothing. On that Saturday afternoon as people were coming in and buying up all the good bargains, a neighbor who was in graduate school studying psychology came in and asked if she could speak to me for a few minutes. When everyone left, she closed the door to my apartment and after buying the only original watercolor I owned for $25, she asked,

"What are you doing? Why are you selling everything?"

I told her about the darkness I was living in and that I had to end it.

"You're going to get better. This despair will pass. Please stop selling all your things. Close the door and stop."

I didn't believe her, but I listened to her. I think now that God was speaking to me through her. I closed the door and sat there in my apartment realizing I had lost the ability to manage my life. I longed for someone to come in and take charge. I wasn't doing such a good job. I could no longer make logical decisions. I needed a mother.

My mother, who was still living in southern Illinois, was very concerned about me. She called me every day, and all I could say was,

"I'm going to kill myself today."

She invited me to come back home for a while and stay with her. I wasn't interested. Every day I wandered around aimlessly like a lost child. One day I'd begin a project and the next day I'd abandon it and start another one – none of them lasted longer than a day.

One day I found myself at a church service and it was there that I met Carol. I guess I went to church because I was longing for some kind of spiritual connection. Carol became my friend and on some of my most difficult days, she'd invite me over to her house and take care of me. She'd cook for me, listen to me ramble on and take me for walks and outings with her.

I began seeing a therapist I found through the Army's insurance program. After three months of weekly visits, she diagnosed me as being "clinically depressed" and referred me to a psychiatrist. When I told her I was reluctant to see a psychiatrist, she challenged me,

"Are you afraid he'll recommend hospitalization?"

Just to show her I wasn't, I agreed to go. The night before the scheduled appointment, I was anxious so I called my friend Susan who invited me to come over and spend the night at her house. Susan was very loving and supportive – a true oasis from my madness. She was breast-feeding her newborn daughter. Her home contained all that was lacking in my life. It was lovely – neat, orderly, and filled with joy. She and her husband, Lowell, were not frightened by my insanity as many of my other friends were.

My friends in Werner's network didn't understand what I was going through. They kept telling me to pull myself together and get on with my life. It was unsettling for them to see the powerful person I had been be rendered so ineffectual. Why wasn't I using all I had learned in my thirteen years with Werner to pull myself up by the bootstraps? My illness frightened them. They had no context to fit it into.

My brief meeting with the psychiatrist angered me. He sat in the corner of his office wearing his tinted glasses, his legs crossed with his pad and pencil on his lap. After about five questions, he handled me a prescription for Prozac and bid me farewell. The meeting lasted about five minutes. A few days later I got a bill for $120.00.

I was appalled by his insensitivity. I felt like an animal that had been diagnosed by a veterinarian. I felt absolutely no compassion or empathy from him. I had a lot of questions which I didn't even have the opportunity to ask because the time was so limited. I found out later this particular type of appointment is called a medication appointment and isn't meant to be a full session of therapy.

With so many unanswered questions I stumbled over to the public library and checked out several books about depression. I found there was a name for the condition I was experiencing and that I'd get over it eventually. Many people had. It wasn't just my sickness – others suffered from it too. There was a name for "the descent into hell" I was experiencing. It was called a "clinical depression".

I had developed a prejudice against anti-depressant drugs while working for Werner. His organization screened people carefully and often didn't allow people who had a history of taking medication for any psychiatric illness to take courses. I didn't want to admit I was unstable and needed medication. I didn't want the stigma attached to mental illness.

I attempted to cure my depression by exercising and positive thinking. I contacted the Huxley Institute who offered me doctors who treated patients without medication, but the path was long and arduous and nearly as expensive as the psychiatrist. Living in extreme panic and anxiety, the non-drug route didn't seem like it could save me fast enough. I thought I would die before I got better. For a while after I exercised, I'd feel better, but I couldn't exercise enough to quiet the monster that was inhabiting my mind.

Grief Denied

Overwhelmed, I sank deeper and deeper into the abyss, spending more and more time planning the details of my departure.

Dr. Caldwell, the Army psychiatrist, called it a "major depressive episode." I was so filled with rage that I turned against myself and began to plan my suicide. To just disappear without any mess would be ideal. To simply not be on the planet. It seemed simple enough. But what was I to do with this body? How could I do it without leaving a mess for somebody else, namely my daughter, to deal with?

My friend Roy did it. He jumped off the Golden Gate Bridge and his body was never found. No one had to see him dead. His friends and relatives just had to imagine like I did when Howard died – to imagine what his dead body looked like.

His two sons, 11 and 13, had no explanation – he just disappeared one day – they found his car parked near the Golden Gate Bridge with his glasses, his wallet and his bottle of antidepressants on the front seat. No body to deal with, no mess, no note explaining why.

It can't be explained: war, death, depression, suicide – it can't be explained – no way. There isn't a note that's long enough to say it all.

My friend, Roy, was a Vietnam vet.

One afternoon, while sitting on the floor in my bedroom staring out the window into the abyss of my mind, and entertaining thoughts of suicide, I grabbed Michelle's stuffed monkey, Wendy, which was perched on my dresser. I ripped its arms and legs off and ripped its stomach open. When this episode of rage was over,

I realized I had just destroyed a gift I had given Michelle for Valentine's Day when she was 8 years old. I was scared that day. Intuitively, I knew I could be the next object of my rage.

I told Michelle repeatedly during this period that I had lost hope and wanted to die. She was the only human being I still had a connection with. I had withdrawn from my friends and completely split with Tom. I couldn't handle what little demands he made on me, and he represented yet another issue to be depressed about – my inability to maintain a satisfying, intimate relationship with a man.

I repeatedly called Michelle at work just to connect with another human being. She had a job that didn't allow her to receive personal phone calls. I called anyway.

During this time I didn't write. I was so out of touch with myself, I didn't even keep a journal. Journals have always been my companions, my shelters during the storms of my life. Without them, I would have died years ago. They have guided me to my truth time and time again. Not keeping a journal during this time indicated how invaded I was by depression.

One day when Michelle and I were driving down the road to her house, I began the same old ruminating about how I didn't want to live another day longer. She finally got fed up,

"If you want to die, go ahead. I can't save you. But just remember one thing, you can't change your mind. Death is permanent. You won't be here when I get married, and you won't be here when I have a baby." She released me – gave me permission to die. I was initially stunned by what she had said, but I think it jarred me into taking some positive action.

One of the symptoms of my depression was disturbed sleep patterns. Each morning at about 3 a.m. I'd awake and start ruminating. I couldn't get back to sleep, so I'd lie there and fall victim to the endless repetition of negative, nasty thoughts about myself. It was hell. Death seemed like the only way out.

One Monday morning after spending the weekend with Michelle, I dropped her off at work and silently said my goodbyes – my final goodbyes. I never told her, of course, but I was thinking,

"This is it – the last time I'll see you."

My plans were to go home, fill the bathtub with water and get in with the hair dryer plugged in and turned on. I find it rather ironic that I was going to kill myself in the bathtub which is now one of my favorite ways to nurture myself – long, hot bubble baths with candlelight and soft soothing music.

My friend Valerie was scheduled to come over to buy a bookshelf at 6 p.m. that day. She would be the one to find my body.

The trip from Michelle's work to my apartment took an hour and a half. Thank God. Some little spark of me didn't want to die and took the time to consider the repercussions of my act – the police, the note, someone would call Michelle. She'd come, identify my body – her life would be destroyed. I couldn't destroy her life. Despite my own personal despair, I couldn't take my life knowing the chaos it would create in hers. I loved her too much.

That realization was a turning point. Immediately following Howard's death I wanted to die, but I had to continue because I was carrying a child and that child deserved a chance at life. Now I had to continue because my suicide would emotionally destroy that child. Twice Michelle has saved my life.

And so began the slow, steady climb back to health. A few days later while kneeling on the floor at the foot of my bed and sobbing, it suddenly occurred to me to call the psychiatric department at the local Army hospital and make an appointment with a psychiatrist. I dialed the number and made an appointment. It was August 1990. I had been in this hell for five months.

Dr. Caldwell, the army psychiatrist, spent an hour with me. When he learned about my job with Werner Erhard, he asked me if I had seen the special that had just aired on "60 Minutes" about Werner. One of his daughters stated that he had sexually abused her and that he was responsible for abusing his second wife. Dr. Caldwell asked me about any abuse I had experienced in the organization. I told him about the last position I had held.

He also asked me about my childhood and if there was any alcoholism in my family. I told him my father was an alcoholic who had died at 62.

Grief Denied

At the end of the session, Dr. Caldwell gave me a prescription for an anti-depressant. He explained that my seratonin level was depleted and that these pills would boost the production of that hormone and help me to feel like myself again. He took the time to explain it all to me unlike the previous psychiatrist who had just handed me a prescription. I got the prescription filled and started taking the pills. I trusted Dr. Caldwell and surrendered to his recommendation. I had to. I had decided to live and needed to take whatever measures I could to get well.

A few weeks later, my friends, Susan and Lowell Cable, invited me to go with them and their infant daughter on an adventure in their motor home. I thought perhaps traveling with them would change my perspective so I went, but I became a burden. It's difficult to be around a depressed person. With my constant ruminating, I think I dragged them down into the despair with me. Susan told me years later that she and Lowell invited me to go with them to keep me from killing myself.

Susan went with me to see Dr. Caldwell before we left on the trip. To ensure that I didn't take an overdose of the anti-depressants, Dr. Caldwell put her in charge of dispensing my medication on the trip. I felt so humiliated to have someone else in charge like that. It was a clear indication of how unstable I was.

It soon became apparent that traveling with them wasn't solving anything. I was just running away. I couldn't let myself relax and enjoy the trip.

When I was depressed, every task seemed insurmountable. I had moved all the way across the country two different times – from Illinois to Denver and then from Denver to California, yet the move out of my small apartment seemed impossible. I ruminated about it constantly.

Susan and Lowell helped me clean the apartment and move my furniture into a storage unit in Lake County, close to where Michelle was living with Scott. I showed up on Michelle's doorstep that day and asked if I could stay with her for a while.

The medication Dr. Caldwell gave me didn't help. After taking it for several months, I was still depressed. So in January of 1991 he weaned me off that anti-depressant and started me on another. He explained that sometimes it takes a while to find the right medication.

After two weeks on the new medication, I woke up one day with a glimmer of hope. I was so thankful. I recognized hope – I used to wake up with it everyday. It was coming back. I was thrilled.

After not working for nine months, I got a job as a retail clerk in an office supply store in Santa Rosa. It was a forty-five minute drive from Michelle and Scott's house, which included driving over two mountain ranges. I thought living with Michelle and Scott would be good for me, but it soon became obvious it wasn't working for any of us so I found a house to share with two other single women in Rohnert Park. I was still somewhat depressed but I hoped it wasn't obvious. I spent most of my time in my bedroom, which was adjacent to the big kitchen we all shared. I always kept my door closed and went to bed every night at 8 p.m. Because the anti-depressants hyped me up, I had to take a sleeping pill to get to sleep. I felt I was existing on pills. I was.

Many nights in that house in Rohnert Park, I'd soak in the bathtub and listen to an audio tape by Kirtana called *Healing Rain*. Music was one of the few comforts I found during my depression.

The lyrics of her song, *Healing Rain*

> *In a dream that's left for dead,*
> *in a heart that's closed from pain,*
> *all it takes is a light from the spirit*
> *and a healing rain...*

I listened to this tape over and over again. As the depression subsided, I had increased energy and began to feel ambitious again.

My job as a retail clerk in the office supply store soon became boring. To get back into the swing of things, I enrolled in a course about financial management which was taught by a couple who had been involved in Werner's network. During the eight-week course the owners of the company invited me to come in for an interview to work with them. I was thrilled. I interviewed with the two owners and with each person on their staff but I didn't get the job. I was devastated. I wanted out of the retail clerk job and it must have been obvious because shortly thereafter I got fired. They knew I was looking for another position. I had asked for time-off for the interviews.

So there I was without a job or a romantic relationship, both of which I craved desperately. But this time I didn't panic. It felt as if the universe was trying to nudge me into a new way of defining myself.

✪

For years I thought my addictions were merely bad habits, more evidence that I was defective. I wondered why I had so many. It wasn't until I realized that they were the means by which I coped with the difficult circumstances in my life that I could begin to have some compassion for myself.

Alcohol was the first substance I used to mask the pain. I was never a fall-down drunk like my father, but I had to have a glass or two of wine every evening with my meal to take the edge off the day. When friends came over, the drinking continued until the bottle or several were empty.

One morning, when I was living in Denver, I woke up and didn't remember how I had gotten home the night before. I remembered drinking beer, wine and tequila in City Park, but the rest of the evening was a blur. I stopped drinking shortly after that. I never went to a recovery program for help. I just did it on my own – by self-will.

Overworking was the next escape I used. When I worked for Werner, I worked approximately 70 hours a week. Being so busy kept my pain submerged.

Grief Denied

My most insidious addiction, however, was to love and sex. I used affairs with men, just as I had used alcohol and overworking, in an attempt to heal the wounds of loss. I couldn't be without a man for very long. Sometimes I'd resort to extreme measures – like going to bars to find one.

Anyone who has battled with an addiction knows the push and pull of the substance. You can't continue to use because you see how it's harming you, but you also think you can't live without it. I repeatedly injured myself with men – either by betraying them or being betrayed by them. The cycle continued for years.

I stopped the addictive cycle with men when I broke up with Tom. My relationship with him had started out so sweetly and ended so bitterly, I just couldn't engage in the process any longer. It was too painful.

Whenever I'd realize I was engaged in another addiction, I'd just stop it. I had a strong will. So I stopped men too. Cold turkey. It was the hardest addiction to stop. Many days I felt like climbing the walls – like I was going insane.

Someone told me once that trying to manage all our addictions is like trying to put an octopus to bed and cover it with a blanket.

Eventually I hit the addiction I couldn't handle on my own. Thank God.

One morning after an all-day birthday celebration for a friend, I lay in bed with my stomach hurting, and realized I had spent all my time at the party going from one food table to the next. I hadn't even talked to anybody. I thought back further and remembered that when I got dressed to go, I hadn't been able to find the right thing to wear. I had outgrown all my clothes. The only slacks which still fit were a pair of black stretch pants and I wore them everywhere. I had reached an all-time-high with my weight – weighing even more than I did when I was nine months pregnant.

When I broke up with Tom, I turned to food for comfort. What started out as a little extra food on my plate every now and then turned into a nightmare of consistent, compulsive overeating.

My father had destroyed himself with alcohol and I was on the same road of destruction – only my obsession was with food. I realized I couldn't stop this addiction on my own.

However, my relentless self-will doesn't give up easily, so in a final attempt to shrink my stomach and thereby curb my appetite, I decided to fast for five days. I was high during the fast and happy to be relieved of the obsession with food. But how long could I stay on the fast? Not long.

Within a day of breaking the fast, I began compulsive overeating again. It was frightening. I'd never felt so powerless and out of control in my life. I wondered how big I'd get before I exploded.

Hitting bottom with an addiction brings you to your knees. You learn to ask for help – first from a sponsor and then from your God. If you don't have a God, you just make one up.

Grief Denied

When Howard died in Vietnam, I lost faith in God. My God, at the time, was an old man in the sky with a gray beard and a big ledger book in which he recorded all the bad deeds I had done. I couldn't understand what I had done to warrant such drastic punishment – having my husband die in Vietnam.

Somewhere in my young Catholic mind, I believed that if I was good, God would be good to me. Well, I'd been good. I obeyed the ten commandments, I'd remained chaste right up until I was married just as the Catholic church and my mother demanded. How come my God had abandoned me? I couldn't understand.

This childhood God was unpredictable – untrustworthy. As a child I was continually threatened with the wrath of God. He was held over me as a cruel character who would punish me if I was bad. I was always anticipating the next blow to come from God reminding me of my unworthiness.

When things went well for a while, the voice inside me was always saying, "Watch out, something bad is going to happen soon." I'd unconsciously sabotage everything so I could bring more of the tragic fate I thought I deserved upon myself.

In Werner I found a God-like figure who appeared to be a benevolent God initially, but when he needed a sacrificial lamb for one of his managers, he asked me to offer myself up and I did. I could play the part well.

Facing my addictions and asking for help led me to redefine God and to begin to trust again. I always thought that people in recovery programs were victims. I avoided them. They were addicts and I was above all that. Maybe I developed this attitude when working for Werner, or maybe it was my own shame and disgust at watching my father drunk for so many years that caused me to deny a similar problem in myself.

When I couldn't quit eating, I humbly found my way to a recovery program. Initially, all I did at the meetings was cry. I couldn't even speak. I was so ashamed of myself for my inability to stop eating. Such a simple thing and yet I couldn't do it. It was then that I understood and began to have compassion for my father's drinking problem. He could no more stop drinking than I could stop eating.

At the recovery meetings, I found a fellowship of people who were in various stages of breaking denial about their addictions. Most importantly at these meetings, I found a place where I could finally express my feelings. I could cry. I had spent my childhood and my years with Werner learning to put my feelings aside. I didn't have to anymore.

In my quest for a new God, I began to explore some of the New Age churches in my area. At the Church of Religious Science I met Pam Adair, my first spiritual teacher. She taught me how to feel the presence of God. She kept telling me to slow down and sit still. When I did, I could feel surrender happening in my body. It felt as if my long-held stance of determination was softening and melting away. The more and the deeper I was able to surrender, the more joyful and serene my life became.

Grief Denied

I found myself directed to the ways and means by which to continue. Everything in my life led me toward the next step. I witnessed synchronicity of events and willingly surrendered to them.

I began to imagine the existence of a benevolent God. In the beginning, I had to pretend that God was for me and not against me. I didn't have much evidence yet. Pam asked me to do affirmations that good would come to me. I could surrender in her presence and if she said I could trust, maybe I could.

In my search for a new God, I began to imagine being held in the arms of a benevolent Force. Maybe this Force could provide a safety net in which I could surrender and fall apart – really fall apart – the kind of falling apart I had to do to fully grieve. Beginning to trust in this Force allowed me to feel safe enough to surrender to the enormous amount of grief I carried inside me. I didn't develop this trust in a day. It came a little at a time. When each move I made toward surrendering proved to be a safe one, I'd take a little bigger step the next time.

I learned to pray again. I had stopped when Howard died. But now my prayers were different. Instead of asking God to give me all the things I wanted like a great job and a sexy, rich man, I started asking God to show me what my life's purpose was and how to fulfill it. As it turned out, I was shown, but not nearly as succinctly and quickly as I would have liked. So I developed some patience in the process.

Facing my addictions and working a program of recovery allowed me to enter the feelings which had been suppressed for many years. The first feeling to surface was, of course, grief. As I tip-toed into twenty-five years of unresolved grief, I was given the courage to do the things I needed to do to heal.

In response to the difficult circumstances in my life, I had learned to fight and to "go it alone". Moving and changing everything, I had started over so many times in new jobs, in new communities and with new loves, ditching one man and finding another, never letting myself truly love any of them.

If someone had intercepted me when I was doing all that, and said,

"Stop and deal with your grief," I wouldn't have listened. I was strong-willed. I was determined that if I fought hard enough, I could get what I wanted in life. Fighting was my way of coping. So the more losses I had, the harder I fought.

My spiritual growth evolved as I learned to surrender. Giving up the battle I'd always had with life was the beginning of humility, healing and a new concept of God. Many times I'd just sit and cry like an angry child who was admitting defeat because she didn't have any "fight" left in her. For the first time in my life, I admitted powerlessness. It was humiliating, yet very freeing at the same time. As my process of surrendering deepened, I felt ready to discontinue the medication for depression.

So after ten months of taking the second anti-depressant, I wrote Dr. Caldwell a thank-you note and asked him to sign a referral allowing me to work with a civilian therapist in my home town. I was a little scared that I'd slip back into another episode of depression, but I didn't.

After interviewing several therapists, I chose one and with her help began to investigate my past, the past from which I'd been running my whole life. I asked her if I could see her twice a month or whenever I felt like it. She said,

"No, it would be best to meet weekly."

I surrendered again. I'm glad I did. I was grateful to be on my way out of hell.

6. Opening the Box —
Entering the Grief

It was Fall again, the Fall of '92 and I was living alone for the first time in my life. At a Christmas party the previous year, a friend had asked,

"Have you ever lived alone?"

I thought surely I must have, but when I tried to recall the time and the place, I couldn't. There had always been someone with me either physically or psychically. I had spent most of my life in the service of others: parents, friends, employers, boyfriends. Even pets took a lot of care and energy. I became intrigued with the idea of living alone without any distractions. I wanted to learn to be selfish. I thought it might be good for a change.

The perfect place found me one day. I was on my way to the gym when I saw a small apartment complex in the northwest part of Santa Rosa. The thing that intrigued me was the row of weeping willows in front. As a child I had a weeping willow in my back yard and would often sit in its shade when I didn't know where else to go for comfort.

The tree of my childhood was a tall, gentle woman whose long, flowing hair provided safety and shelter where I could hide. This small apartment complex had a whole row of these tall, gentle women inviting me to seek sanctuary – a sacred place to heal.

The manager, John, a friendly sort of a guy, greeted me as I drove in the driveway.

"I'm the best apartment manager in the city," he said as he showed me the one-bedroom apartment. I asked him if I could be alone in the apartment for a few minutes. I browsed around in the two rooms to get a sense of the place. It felt like home, cozy, quiet and most importantly, safe. The bedroom had a sliding glass door that opened onto a private patio with a patch of soil where I could plant a vegetable garden. The living room had a window which framed the willows.

I moved into the apartment two weeks later and in the process came across the box marked, "Vietnam." The old familiar feelings arose – despair, regret, and sorrow – feelings I had avoided for twenty-five years. The box was a reminder of a life I struggled to forget but its contents haunted me.

I was taken back to the day in June of '68 when a slip in my mom's post office box indicated that there was a parcel waiting at the counter. When I went to the window, they handed me the box, which I then carried several blocks to my parents' home. I was eight months pregnant.

As I opened it, the first thing I noticed was the smell – a very distinct smell – a moldy, damp smell like the smell in the basement of my mom's house. I slowly explored the contents of the box.

A Vietnam Widow's Story

All the letters and audio tapes he had received during his short two-month tour were in the box. Howard's wallet and everything in it was soaked, including the Sacred Heart Scapula given to him by his grandmother, Marie. His I.D.s and photos were ruined. They told me he was crossing a bridge over a canal, assaulting a machine gun position when he died. I guess he was carrying his wallet. Maybe he fell in the canal. I tried to imagine the scene of his death, but nothing came. I just couldn't imagine it.

I picked up a small box. When I opened it, his wedding ring came tumbling out and landed on the gold, sculptured carpet of my mom's living room floor. My heart sank. In that moment, his death was confirmed. He wouldn't let anyone have his wedding ring unless he was dead.

I felt disgust, the kind that comes with untimely death. These moldy remnants of a life that used to be were all I had left. There were military orders, socks, shoes, and underwear. And of course, there was the administration guarantee he received when he enlisted in the Army; it promised him an administrative job.

I didn't know where his dog tags were, they weren't in the box. Maybe they were in his coffin. I couldn't sit with this box for very long. I was so angry with the Army and my country for sending him to die in an undeclared war.

I taped the box shut and kept it hidden under beds, in the back of closets, away from view in the same way that I kept all the feelings associated with this box hidden. Each time I moved, which was quite often, I'd come across the box. I'd look at it momentarily and then quickly shove it into the next hiding place. I dared not venture into the box for fear it would swallow me up. With each move, the avoidance grew stronger.

Once while I was living at the 6-Day Course, when I moved from one staff house to another, one of the staff members who helped me move asked me why I was saving the Vietnam box. She advised me,

"Get rid of it, burn it. It's the past, forget it, move on. Why are you still dwelling on Vietnam?"

This type of comment was pretty common around Werner's network. The past and any feelings associated with it were to be put aside.

Thank God I didn't take her advice. I didn't know it then, but the box contained the items I needed to help me heal.

As courageous as I was in all other aspects of my life, I avoided this box and the grief it contained at all costs. I kept trying "to put it behind me" as President Ford had advised the veterans to do. But shoving that box and my feelings away year after year only postponed my life, it didn't further it.

In a final attempt to expel my dead husband from my life, I asked Michelle if she wanted the "Vietnam" box. She gladly took it. It was all she had of her father.

A few weeks later on Father's Day, when Michelle was 24 years old, the same age her father was when he died, she, for the first time, ventured into the box and read the letters her father had written when he was in Vietnam.

He referred to her as "the little seed." Michelle listened to the audio tape in which he said he had considered buying a teddy bear for her at the PX, but had decided to wait until the following month. By then, he was already dead.

A few months later in mid-November, an incident occurred that prompted me to open the box and begin to explore its contents. I had invited Michelle and Scott over for dinner. Thanksgiving was approaching and I knew they would be celebrating the holiday with Scott's relatives, so I planned an early Thanksgiving celebration for just the three of us. I got out the fine china, the linens, the crystal and made room in my tiny place for the three of us to sit down and have dinner together.

On that Friday evening Michelle and Scott showed up at my door giggling and acting silly. They continued giggling when I asked,"What's going on?" Scott handed me his camera, "Would you take a picture of us?" he asked. I could tell they had something up their sleeves. Scott seemed particularly nervous.

After a while I noticed that Michelle had her left hand in her jean pocket. "Do you have something on your left hand to show me?" I finally asked. She giggled again, pulled her hand out of her pocket and displayed a stunning emerald-cut diamond.

"We're engaged."

Scott looked at me sheepishly and said "I hope it's okay." I hugged them both as tears streamed down my cheeks.

"I guess instead of celebrating Thanksgiving, we'll celebrate your engagement," I said.

As we sat down at the dinner table that evening, the old familiar feeling arose – someone was missing on this momentous occasion. Of course, he had been missing from all those special moments in her life – her birth, her first day of school, the day she got her driver's license, her first date, her high school graduation and now her engagement. Somehow it didn't seem possible that he would miss her marriage too. And so we had yet another celebration where there was no husband, no father, just silence and an empty chair at our dining room table.

Michelle and Scott decided to get married the following June, so we began planning the wedding immediately. The first stop was the bridal shop, *Brides and Maids,* an old Victorian home converted into a salon which contained all the fixings for a lovely June wedding. As we climbed the steps to the shop, I felt both excited and scared.

Michelle had picked out the dress she wanted from a bridal magazine. When she showed the dress to the sales clerk, she was excited to find they actually had it. Michelle has exquisite taste. She usually likes the most expensive item on the rack. She likes what she likes and rarely settles for less. She'd rather do without. Her father was like that also. His Hamilton watch never came back from Vietnam. I don't know what happened to it.

She was swept off by the sales clerk into a huge dressing room with the dress, a strapless bra, a big fluffy slip and a pair of borrowed high heel shoes. I wandered around in a daze looking at the dresses for the mother-of-the-bride.

When Michelle came out in the wedding dress and stood on the pedestal in front of the full-length three-way mirror, I was stunned. There standing before me was my baby – now a beautiful woman in a bridal gown. Where had her childhood gone? How had she grown up so fast? What did all this mean?

I was taken back to the day when I had first put on a wedding gown. The tears came. I couldn't stop them.

"What do you think, Mom?" I was brought back to reality.

"What do you think of the dress?"

"It's beautiful," was all I could say. The tears continued to fall as I remembered the joy with which I planned my wedding and the tragedy that occurred so shortly thereafter. I was away in my thoughts and missed a great deal of what was happening in the bridal salon that day. Michelle was embarrassed that I was crying. She's often embarrassed by me. She always wanted me to be normal – whatever that means. I guess normal means a family that consists of a mom, a dad and some sisters and brothers.

In high school her best friend, Marie Meany, had a large family and Michelle spent most of her high school years at the Meany household hanging out with Marie's parents and siblings. I missed her, but knew it was what she needed and wanted, a big family. Since I didn't remarry and have more children she never got the big family she wanted. Now she was planning to begin her own family and was determined that she'd have more than one child.

Michelle told me on the way home from the bridal shop about the father who was helping his daughter pick out a dress in the adjoining room. He was telling her how beautiful she looked. We were both in tears when she dropped me off at my apartment that day.

The following week we went to see Steve Martin's movie, *Father of the Bride*. I thought it was funny and laughed hysterically. Scott told me later Michelle cried all the way home. As her wedding approached, she and I were both painfully aware of the blank space that had been in our lives for so many years – an empty chair, a silent voice, all where a father was supposed to be.

Planning Michelle's wedding was the catalyst for me to address my unresolved grief. Each event related to the wedding left me in tears. One day Michelle asked me to walk her down the aisle. I was speechless. My mother had always told me,

"When Michelle gets married, her godfather, Stan, will walk her down the aisle."

I just assumed that's what would happen. When I questioned Michelle about asking her uncle to do it, she said,

"You raised me. Why would I have him walk me down the aisle?"

I told Michelle I didn't believe in the concept of giving her away. She said she didn't see it that way. She saw it simply as changing partners in life. I had been her partner throughout her childhood and she was now going to be with her new partner, her husband. I had always hoped that I had raised her to be a feminist and when she asked me to walk her down the aisle, I knew I had succeeded. The equality I've struggled so hard to achieve is ingrained in her.

In the solitude of my quiet sanctuary, every time I imagined walking her down the aisle, I sobbed. This precious gift Howard left with me was going off to begin her life with her husband. She would no longer be with me. Even though Michelle and Scott had been living together for a couple years, their wedding marked a rite of passage that I felt would change my relationship with her forever.

As the wedding drew closer and the plans took more definite shape, I asked Michelle if we could have a photo of her father at the wedding. "Could we offer a toast in his honor?" I asked.

It seemed so important to me that he be acknowledged that day. She didn't want to have her father mentioned. That broke my heart. I wanted all the guests to know him – to know that he was the other parent of this precious young woman who was getting married.

Grief Denied

Michelle didn't want any sadness on her wedding day. "We all know my dad will be with us in spirit that day, we don't have to mention it," she said.

Michelle is a very private person. She doesn't as readily hang her laundry out on the line to dry as I do.

Early in the morning of her wedding day when she and her bridesmaids were on their way to the salon to get their hair and makeup done, she asked her bridesmaids,

"Do you think my dad can see me today?"

I felt strongly that he or at least a symbol of him had to be there on her wedding day. This was the one event it seemed he couldn't miss. He had to be there to dance with me during the parents' dance, to console me because our only child was leaving home, and to assure me that he would be there with me in the second half of my life to grow old with me.

I cried every day during the six months of wedding planning. I lived alone so I had no one to tell me to stop. I began to write as a way of sorting out my feelings.

In writing I finally found a container which could hold my grief. As I spent more and more time writing, I encountered more and more grief. The blank page wanted to hear it all – every last detail. It never told me "stop crying" or "you should be over it by now." It just sat with me in the silence of my grief. The tears poured out.

I didn't have to swallow my sorrow anymore. I felt blessed to have found such a strong witness to help me get through the darkness I was facing.

When that special day came and we began the symbolic march down the aisle, I felt Howard's presence with us. I didn't cry. I was beaming like a proud peacock showing all its tail feathers. Friends told me later that there seemed to be a glow emanating from Michelle and me as we walked down the aisle. Nearly all the guests had tears in their eyes – particularly those who had known her father. The sight of a mother walking a bride down the aisle is a bold statement – someone is missing.

There have been so few times in my life when I've actually been present in the moment. The experience of walking Michelle down the aisle contained some of those precious moments. My heart was pounding, my beautiful daughter was next to me in layers of lace, hair all puffed up, nails long and painted white, smelling of her favorite perfume, Paris. The whole arbor was filled with guests waiting to see us walk down the aisle. Michelle carried her exquisite arrangement of flowers and a white handkerchief my mother had embroidered for her. She grabbed my arm.

"I think I am going to faint, Mom," she said.

I whispered, "Just breathe."

We began the symbolic journey. Scott stood waiting wide-eyed at the end of the aisle all dressed up in a black tuxedo with tails. I'd never seen such a look of astonishment and wonder on his face as he had that day. He looked as if he had just seen God.

I wanted to walk slowly. I wanted the walk to never end. I wanted time to remember her childhood, her teenage years, her young adulthood. I wanted time for all the world to see her – to look at this beautiful child of mine who was so happy, so willing and so ready to embark on the journey of marriage.

A beginning for her – and a beginning and an ending for me. The end of having her body and soul in my care and keeping, and the beginning of opportunities for me to explore the perimeters of my own soul.

When we arrived where Scott and the rest of the wedding party were waiting, I hugged and kissed Michelle, and when I hugged Scott, I whispered in his ear,

"Take good care of my baby."

I walked away and sat in the first row, next to my loyal mother, the one who was there when I birthed her, the one who was there on special occasions when her father wasn't. She always played a significant role in Michelle's life. Even though she has fifteen other grandchildren, Michelle is special to her. I guess because I was living with Mom when Michelle was born and then she came to live with us and cared for Michelle when I finished my last two years of college.

Mom often says, "Those were the happiest days of my life when I was caring for Michelle, and you were in college."

Michelle spent a month with Mom every summer throughout her grade school years. Sometimes I'm jealous of the bond between them. It seems to me that my mother loves Michelle in a way she could never love me.

"We are gathered here today to join Michelle and Scott in the sacred bond of matrimony."

The tears came. I was out of the spotlight now, I could cry.

Howard's sister, Connie, her husband, Allen, and their son, Billy, were the only relatives from Howard's side of the family who came to the wedding. I was disappointed that Howard's parents didn't come. They said they weren't well enough to make the trip. The lack of relatives from his side of the family compounded his absence that day.

Looking back now, I see that I was in a trance. I greeted guests, played the Mother-of-the-Bride role very well, but mostly I was turned deep within.

After the best man gave the toast for the bride and groom, Scott took the microphone and began to tell Michelle how much he loved her. Right there in front of all the guests, he spoke of the depths of his love for her. I'd never seen a man do that before. Michelle, her bridesmaids, I and many of the guests cried as he spoke.

For their first dance, Michelle and Scott chose the song, *All My Life*, written by Karla Bonhoff.

> *Am I really here in your arms?*
> *It's just like I dreamed it would be.*
>
> *Feel like we're frozen in time*
> *You're the only one I can see*
>
> *Hey, I've looked all my life for you, now you're here.*
> *Hey, I'll spend all my life with you - all my life.*
>
> *And I never really knew how to love,*
> *I just hoped somehow I'd see -*
> *asked for a little help from above -*
> *send an angel down to me............*
>
> *Never thought that I could feel a love so tender*
> *Never thought I could let those feelings show.*
>
> *But now my heart is on my sleeve and this love will never*
> *leave, I know, I know.........*

I stood on the sidelines sobbing as I witnessed the two of them swaying in each others arms under the grape arbor, looking each other in the eye as they danced, uninhibited by their audience. When I turned to run and find a place to cry, I bumped into my mom who grabbed me. As we embraced and wept in each other's arms, I whispered to Mom,

"Aren't you glad she's so happy?"

All a parent ever wants for their child is happiness and there we were, Michelle's two parents, embracing and weeping, both for her happiness and for our sadness about losing our little girl. As I stood there with Mom, I remembered my wedding day. When Howard and I had packed our U-Haul at the end of the day and were ready to leave for Fort Benning, Mom grabbed Howard and starting sobbing in his arms.

When it came time for the parents' dance, I looked around to find someone to dance with and was met by my girlfriend, Kathy, offering her husband, Frank, as my partner. Kathy was the friend who had invited me to live with her in Chicago the summer I met Howard. And Michelle had been the flower girl at Kathy and Frank's wedding on the Big Sur coast in 1975.

Frank and I danced the parents' dance. I thought later I should have danced with my mother. She, more than anyone else, was Michelle's other parent. When Michelle couldn't talk to me, or get what she wanted from me, she'd call her grandma.

At the end of the day, after the cake had been cut, and the toast to the bride and groom was over, Michelle and Scott gathered with their friends and wedding party to plan where and how they would continue the celebration.

Grief Denied

I stood looking on, feeling lost and alone, much as I felt at the end of the day we buried Howard at Oak Ridge Cemetery in Springfield, Illinois.

Michelle's wedding day was different however, I didn't have a life growing inside of me as I did at the funeral. I was really alone for the first time since Howard's death.

Michelle caught a glimpse of me out of the corner of her eye and came over and hugged me and said,

"Mom, don't worry, our relationship won't change that much. Maybe we'll even be closer."

I smiled and hugged her, knowing she couldn't comprehend my loss, or fix it, even though she wanted to.

That day as I left the reception and drove down the winding country road, alone as never before, I felt as if I had been hollowed out by a big scoop. Yet as painful as it was, I was grateful for I knew I was regaining my ability to feel and I was beginning to let go of the two people I had loved more than any others in my life.

7. Give Sorrow Words

A few days after the wedding, all the relatives left, Michelle and Scott went to Disneyland on their honeymoon, and I became very busy again. The old familiar habit kicked in – the survival mechanism which had gotten me through all those years without grieving. I was certain the grieving was over. After all, I had cried every day for the past six months.

In pursuit of my interest in public speaking, I attended a monthly meeting of the National Speakers Association. That particular day they were having an Art Auction. I wandered into the room to see if there was anything that caught my eye. I found a book entitled, *"The Courage To Grieve"* by Judy Tatelbaum. I put a bid on the book and ended up getting it, not by accident, I'm sure.

Opening that book was like opening Howard's coffin. I found that I hadn't even begun to touch the deep-seated grief I carried inside me.

A week later I had the following dream:

I was waiting in the sidelines of an old theater while an announcer was introducing me to the audience. I was going to give a presentation. The theater was old, the house was packed and I was excited. I had made it. I was feeling quite smug and accomplished.

Grief Denied

While waiting there I glanced up into the rafters and saw a dirty, wild-looking little girl. She was barefoot and filthy. Her hair was matted, her whole body full of nicks, cuts and bruises.

She was maneuvering a big antique trunk around. When I saw what she was attempting to do (push the trunk over the edge of the rafter) I began pleading with her, "Please don't push that trunk over the edge. I'm about to give an important presentation."

She gave me a determined look – as if she knew more about the situation than I did. I felt completely powerless. I knew I couldn't convince her to stop.

Just at the moment the announcer completed my introduction, and I walked out in front of the podium and felt the heat of the lights on my face, the little wild child pushed the trunk over onto me. When it hit me, I shattered into a million pieces of glass. I literally disappeared.

I woke up startled. Such an odd feeling – to simply disappear – nothing left but a million pieces of glass. I couldn't get back to sleep that night and was in somewhat of a trance for the next few days. Who was this part of myself that I had not yet faced? It seemed that my task was to embrace this wild child. She'd been in hiding even longer than the Vietnam widow.

The urge to write grew stronger – something wanted to come through. I could no longer ignore such a strong instinctive urge so I slowly let go of what I thought I had to do to survive, and I begin writing full time.

A Vietnam Widow's Story

My apartment was so small, I felt as if I were living in a cocoon. For the first time in my life, I starting giving myself the loving attention I had always given others. Under the sweet flowing branches of my weeping willows, I wrapped my arms around myself and I cried. Tip-toeing very slowly into deeper and deeper periods of introspection, I began to spend more and more time alone, befriending my grief. I stopped eating meat, began meditating, and started walking in the country every day.

Denial was a powerful defense mechanism that had helped me survive for many years. But it was no longer useful to me. As I looked deeper at the depth of despair and pain in my life, I found the strength to face it. I asked my daughter to return the box labeled "Vietnam." I knew I had to open it and look inside. I had to face those feelings.

Michelle brought the box labeled "Vietnam" to my apartment today. It sits in the middle of my living room like an unwanted visitor. It's taking up space, lots of space, physical as well as psychic space. When I open the box to get a glimpse of the insides, I notice the odor. It's as if his dead body is in there. It's time to bury him, but I can't bury him until I feel this shattering pain. His body is long gone, but he remains in my psyche. This box contains the letters, the audio tapes, including the one stamped "Confirmed deceased, return to sender."

When Michelle saw it, she said, "He never heard this one, Mom" and I felt the knot in my stomach which has been there for twenty-five years. I want to vomit out that knot. When the box came back from Vietnam, I stuffed it away and tried to forget. I eventually unloaded it on my daughter, yet I'm not free of it and won't be until I open it, read each letter, listen to his voice on audio tape and feel all the feelings I couldn't feel back in May of '68.

In the box are photographs taken in our house in Columbia, South Carolina: a photograph of me pregnant, cooking dinner, another of Howard wrestling with the dog. These take me back to another lifetime. I'm beginning to open the past and dissect it piece by piece, letter by letter.

Every year Chapter #223 of Vietnam Veterans of America has a booth at the Health and Harmony Festival in my town. Each year when I saw the booth, I'd run the other way as fast as I could. During the summer following Michelle's wedding, I finally had the courage to approach the booth and identify myself as a Vietnam widow.

Later that week, I told my therapist I wanted to talk to those veterans about my experience of being a Vietnam widow.

"When do you think you'll do it?" she asked.

"I'll do it when I get better."

"When might that be?"

I was speechless. It had been twenty-five years – how come I wasn't better? When would I be? Early the following morning I called

VVA's local office. The man who answered the phone said I needed to go before the Board of Directors to get permission to come and tell my story at a general meeting of the membership.

A few nights later I walked into the board meeting terrified. I felt as if I were coming face-to-face with Howard. The meeting was held in a room filled with photos of veterans. It felt like a tomb. I wondered if all those photos on the wall were of dead soldiers. The president of the Board approved my talk and asked me to come the following Tuesday. That was a little sooner than I had expected.

There were only a few veterans present the night I spoke. I could see the anguish on their faces as I told my story. A few were wiping tears, others were looking away, maybe in an attempt to get away from what I was saying. Some of them had watched their buddies die in Vietnam, but had never come face-to-face with a Vietnam widow. I knew it was painful for them to be reminded of Vietnam and to hear about the isolation my daughter and I have lived with for many years. At the end of my talk, they welcomed me home and asked me to join their organization as an associate member.

I regained a little bit of myself after that talk. I had finally broken the isolation and the silence of being a Vietnam widow. I felt a strong urge to keep talking about it – to find more people to tell. And, of course, I was given the opportunity.

The members of Chapter #223 told me about an organization called "Sons and Daughters in Touch." The members are young adults whose fathers were lost or are missing as a result of the Vietnam War. The organization was founded by Tony Cordero and Wanda Ruffin. Tony was only four years old when his dad was missing in action and almost eight years old when his father's remains were returned for the funeral. Wanda Ruffin is a Vietnam widow.

SDIT was having a gathering the following month in Sacramento. I was so excited I immediately called Michelle and asked her to go. She said she was busy that weekend, so I went by myself.

At that gathering I met young men and women who share the same loss as Michelle. When they found out I was a Vietnam widow, some of them were eager to speak with me because their mothers wouldn't talk to them about their fathers or the war. Some of them had been admonished for even approaching the subject. Before joining the organization, most of them had never talked to anyone else who knew what it was like to grow up with the mystery of a man who was their father. Many of them spoke of the identity crisis they suffer when they approach the age at which their fathers died.

One young man told me, "It never seems to end. You keep re-experiencing the loss in different ways for the rest of your life."

When people asked if Michelle's father and I were divorced, I'd stumble around, trying to avoid an answer, because I knew when I told them he died in the Vietnam war, the response I'd get would make me very uncomfortable.

A Vietnam Widow's Story

These young adults spoke of how they had always felt isolated in their own unique form of grief. I could see the close bond that had developed among them and I hoped that at some point, Michelle would join them. I listened to stories about their struggle to define themselves by finding out about the dads they never knew. Any information was precious to them. I was inspired by the measures some of them had taken to find veterans who had served with their fathers.

One young woman told me about an audio tape of her father which she had received two years ago but had never been able to listen to. Another young man had been given an audio tape of his father which he took to his room and listened to over and over again, attempting to make his voice sound like that of his father's.

Coming out of isolation was good for me, but often difficult for the people who heard my story. I learned to stop protecting them and to finally honor the voice of the young widow inside me.

Jonathan Shay in his book entitled, *Achilles in Vietnam* states,

> *"Any blow in life will have longer lasting and more serious consequences if there is no opportunity to communalize it."*

Thank God, I had begun to communalize my grief. I had chosen the local chapter of Vietnam Veterans of America as my first audience because I felt they would be more sympathetic than most.

Grief Denied

That Sunday afternoon as I drove back home I felt a familiar melancholy. It always strikes deepest on Sunday afternoons for some reason. I started composing a letter in my mind, but it soon became too long to remember. I pulled off the shoulder of Highway 80, grabbed the blank book I always carried with me, and wrote the following letter:

Dear Howard:

For twenty-five years I've been dreaming you'd come back. When you did, I wanted to be available to resume where we left off, to discuss our new baby girl, to begin our journey of marriage together. We had so little time to learn about marriage. It got cut short way too soon. I'm beginning to see that I must finally say goodbye. I can't wait for you any longer.

As I finally cry these tears which have been bottled up for so long, I am regaining that 22 year-old maiden that you married. She died when you died. I want her back in my life. In order to get her back, I must experience the grief. I am strong enough now to feel the terror of your death – to open your coffin and look in. I couldn't do it back in '68.

Howard, do you think I'll ever get over you and be normal? I don't. I think the loss of you defined my life.

I've been unable to love as I loved you, afraid to be that open and vulnerable again. You held such a special place in my heart and I haven't been willing to let anyone else in there.

A Vietnam Widow's Story

I've been afraid I'd betray you by loving another. I said "until death do us part" but I never accepted that death had parted us.

As I read your letters one by one, I'm beginning to say goodbye and realize you won't be knocking on my door someday as you've done a thousand times in my dreams. I'm beginning to be able to say goodbye.

A week later, I took the two audio tapes Howard had sent me from Vietnam and went for a walk in Armstrong Woods, a nearby redwood forest. I got all dressed up for this rendezvous with Howard – put on a nice outfit, made up my face and styled my hair. I strapped my portable tape player around my waist, stuck the audio tapes in my backpack and headed for the forest.

Armstrong Woods is a place I often go when I feel lost and scattered. It's a larger-than-life chapel where the redwood trees stretch way up to the sky. When I walk among those giants, I feel safe and sacred as if no harm can come to me. What a perfect place to meet with Howard.

As I walked through the redwood trees listening to his words, I felt his presence with me. I was taken back to '68 when he was sitting on the edge of a bunker. The wind was so strong, he had to get down into the bunker to finish the tape. I could hear the mortar rounds in the background. I was amazed at his ability to joke in the midst of a war. I finished the last audio tape just as I arrived back at my car.

Grief Denied

His final words were:

"Take good care of yourself, the baby and the dog. Remember - you have all my love forever."

Then I heard a round of mortar fire and then silence – the same silence I've lived with for twenty-five years. Those words on the audio tape were all I had left of a lifetime we were going to spend together.

A few days later I came home from a long evening of meditation in which anger towards Howard surfaced for the first time. I was finally leaving denial and moving into the next stage of grief – anger.

I darkened the room, lit two white candles and after rummaging through my closet, found Howard's Army hat which I placed between the two candles. For the first time ever, I began expressing my anger towards my fallen war hero. I sobbed as I beat the floor with my fist finally letting my rage out.

Thanks for coming to visit tonight, Howard. I'm not quite as afraid to talk to you as I used to be. I need to tell you how I'm feeling tonight. I'm tired of glorifying your death – glorifying you as a war hero. I need to tell the truth about your death – about what it was like to have you get on a jet plane one day and never ever come back.

You weren't here to hold my hand and comfort me when I was in labor. God damn it. And you weren't here to celebrate the new being I had brought into the world. The beautiful gorgeous baby that was perfect. You weren't here to share the joy, God damn you, God damn you!

A Vietnam Widow's Story

I've been protecting you for too long. You don't get mad at a war hero. You pretend he's great and he never did anything wrong. But you suffer inside when you do that.

You had no business crossing that bridge and shooting bullets and having bullets shot at you. That's not who you were. Why didn't you recognize that, God damn it!

Some day your daughter will have to do all this grieving also. She's going to be angry with you too. I hope she doesn't wait twenty-five years to have this conversation with you, as I have. Because in twenty-five years a lot of her life will be lost, just as a lot of mine has been lost.

When I asked Michelle to bring the box labeled "Vietnam" back to me, I knew I was dragging your dead body back into my life. I'm much stronger now. I can deal with your dead body. When I was 22 years old and seven months pregnant, I couldn't. I'm finally accepting your death. I know that you aren't going to knock on my door and say you're living some place else. I won't be able to convince you to come back to me. You aren't going to do that. You're gone. The empty space in my life will always be here and I have to quit pretending other-wise. You aren't coming home. You really did die...

Thanks Howie for listening.

My own personal denial of Howard's death was compounded by my country's denial. We all pretended that Vietnam was behind us. But in our silence the war's impact continued to deepen.

Grief Denied

As long as I remained silent I continued to carry the grief. It, therefore, became crucial for me to break the silence and the denial and tell my story to anybody and everybody who would listen.

When Howard went to Vietnam he thought he was fighting communism, but he soon discovered what that war was really about.

In one of his last letters before he was killed, he wrote,

"This war just turns my stomach. It seems like a big political game and I feel that American lives are not to be played with."

A journal entry sums up the way I came to feel about Vietnam:

We destroyed, we killed, we maimed and we did it all in the name of peace. What nonsense – to kill in the pretense of peace – to kill to bring about peace is insane.

My country is insane – its war leaders are insane and I am insane as long as I remain silent.

8. My Fellow Prisoners of War

*Veterans of war
have experience that makes them
the light at the tip of a candle,
illuminating the way of understanding
for those who do not know so well
the causes and results of war, and the way to peace.*

Thich Nhat Hanh

After examining the contents of the Vietnam box, walking in the woods with Howard's audio tapes and getting angry with him, I still wasn't finished. One day when I was speaking with my mom on the phone, she mentioned that she had come across some letters I had written when I was a newlywed.

"I'm going to burn them," she said.

I begged her to send them to me instead. My mother avoids talking about the war and the effect it had on me. She thinks it's best to try to forget. Michelle, who has much more influence with Mom than I do, called her and convinced her to send the letters.

It was a bright, sunny Saturday afternoon when I picked up the letters at my post office box. When I got home, I put my favorite chair in front of the sliding glass doors in my living room and made myself a cup of tea. I was a little anxious about this rendezvous with myself as a 22 year-old military wife.

Grief Denied

Reading the letters was like getting mail from myself twenty-seven years later. Opening each precious one I wasn't sure what I would find. As I read them, I was humbled by the courage of that young Army wife.

In them I spoke of coming to terms with my new life. Howard's training schedule was unpredictable. I'd often have dinner ready at the time he said he'd be home, but he wouldn't show up until hours later. When he finally came home, I'd expect him to spend time with me, but many nights he'd fall asleep on the couch after dinner. I couldn't even wake him to come to bed with me. He was exhausted all the time.

The beginning letters were from Fort Benning, Georgia, where he was in the NCOC Academy training to be a squad leader, and the later ones were from Fort Jackson, South Carolina, where he was an acting squad leader.

I wrote of his increasing fear.

Dear Mom:

Howard is so worried about going to Vietnam. He tries to hide it, but I can tell. He's a nervous wreck. I can't sleep at night because he tosses and turns so much. He knows the time is getting close and really dreads it.

And in the next letter,

I'm really worried about Howard. He hasn't yet faced the fact that he's going to Vietnam. He talks as if we'll be here for a long time. I think he thinks that he won't have to go until after the baby is born.

A Vietnam Widow's Story

We're very happy - even though we're broke and don't have a very happy year to look forward to.

After reading the letters, I wandered down to a nearby video store to rent a movie. The one that jumped out at me was *"Summer of 42."* It wasn't a coincidence that I rented that particular movie. It's about a young woman who lives alone on Cape Cod after her husband goes off to World War II. As I watched her receive the telegram informing her of her husband's death, I saw myself in that role for the first time. The look of terror on her face, the desperate aloneness, and the deep, deep sorrow, I recognized. When the movie was over, I lay on the floor and sobbed. I couldn't move. I don't know how long I lay there. It didn't matter. I dozed off to sleep and eventually went upstairs and again lay on the floor by my bed and sobbed. I don't think I've ever touched such depths of sorrow as I did that night.

I relived the tragic scene and let myself experience the feelings I denied back in '68. I let myself lie on the floor and feel what it felt like to want to die, to give up all hope. I let the feelings come instead of running from them as I had done for years. The next day my eyes were almost swollen shut. I had survived another bout with grief and the sky seemed brighter and bluer than ever before.

I continued to speak at chapter meetings of Vietnam Veterans of America. One night, while driving around alone and lost in downtown Sacramento, looking for the veterans meeting, I pulled off the road, and started crying. I asked myself,

Grief Denied

"Why are you doing this?"

I didn't have an answer. I just felt compelled to follow the urge to continue telling my story. I'd finally given voice to the young war widow and she wanted to tell her story over and over again to make up for the years she'd been silent. One of my friends told me that in other cultures that's how people grieve. They tell and retell their stories of loss to people who listen and care.

I finally found the meeting that night in Sacramento. It was at an American Legion Hall which had an open bar. I had barely begun to tell my story when a couple of veterans in the back of the room left to go have a beer and a cigarette.

Despite the discomfort I often saw in my audiences, I continued to go public with my sorrow, to communalize it. Healing myself became more important than being nice and continuing the silence. I spoke at high schools, university classes, business luncheons, civic organizations – anywhere people would let me come and speak.

In speaking out about my loss, I again experienced the aversion people have to death and grief. Even though I had chosen sympathetic audiences, it became very clear to me that there was an unspoken rule about grief.

Don't do it in public.

It embarrassed people. I think the people most affected are those who have unresolved grief. I think their dormant grief wakes up and asks for expression.

A Vietnam Widow's Story

I was attempting to tell my personal tragedy in a culture that doesn't allow for that kind of expression. Nothing had changed in my twenty-five years of silence – it was still unacceptable to grieve. However, I didn't stop. Continuing the denial was no longer an option. I had tasted the joy on the other side of grief and I wanted more.

Each time I made a presentation, I'd awaken the next morning in tears, releasing more of the piled-up, accumulated grief. Telling the story was excavating the grief. I met people who listened to me talk about my dead husband and cried with me and I met others who walked away.

One Sunday morning a friend called to tell me of an article which was on the front page of my local Sunday paper entitled *"Vietnam Veterans Living in Quiet Affluence."* The article stated that many veterans of the war had come back, gotten on with their lives and were now living in quiet affluence. It even stated an instance in which being in the war had contributed to one man's life immensely. It stated that the majority of Vietnam veterans were well adjusted and affluent.

The article angered me and denied my reality as well as the reality of so many veterans I had met who were battling with the aftermath of that war. I felt invisible again. In anger I sat down and began a letter to the editor. It was so long, it turned out to be a full-length editorial, which was published a few days later:

Grief Denied

The Invisible Casualties of the Vietnam War

Your article in Sunday's edition entitled "Vets Live in Quiet Affluence" was close to home for me.

I am a Vietnam widow who has remained silent for too many years. My husband died in combat on May 10, 1968. He was a squad leader with the 9th Infantry Division. I was 22 years old and 7 months pregnant when his body was escorted back to the states with the instructions, "Non-viewable."

Because Vietnam was such a controversial war — the only war our country has ever lost — I remained silent for all these years. Early on I detected a certain discomfort from people when I told them I was a Vietnam widow. For 25 years I buried my grief and my shame about the war until our daughter announced her wedding plans. When we began planning her wedding, the dam that had been bottled up for all those years broke and the tears began.

I cried throughout the planning of her wedding and am still crying. She got married in June of 1993. The tears did not stop with the wedding; the grief intensified. In September of last year, I finally came out of the closet when I stood before my local chapter of Vietnam Veterans of America and told my story for the first time. I decided to speak to the veterans because I felt it was as close as I could get to speaking to my dead husband. I wanted him to know what it has been like for me. I knew the vets would be sympathetic.

A Vietnam Widow's Story

The veterans told me I was an invisible casualty of the war. They told me I had many of the symptoms of Post-Traumatic Stress Disorder (PTSD) from which many of them suffer. I spoke at other VVA chapters in the Bay Area and learned the only way I am going to heal this wound inside of me is to tell my story over and over for as long as it takes to heal.

I was happy to hear that some veterans are living lives of quiet affluence. Most of the vets I have met since September don't seem to be that fortunate. Many of them are fighting for their lives and many are losing the battle. Since the end of the Vietnam war, it is reported that three times more veterans have taken their own lives than the number of men and women who were killed during the war; Lewis B. Puller, Jr., a decorated Vietnam hero and a Pulitzer prize recipient, being the most recent.

The number of children left fatherless by the war is estimated at 20,000. My daughter, Michelle, who just turned 26, is just beginning to acknowledge her grief about losing her father.

I'd like to sit down and have coffee with the man mentioned in your article who said he cares about children. I'd like to tell him about how my daughter has been affected by losing her father in a war no one understands or wants to talk about. I'd like to tell him about all the issues of unresolved grief she has in her life. Her father died for her freedom. She is not free. She has emotional wounds that need healing and no assistance is available to her as a child of a deceased veteran. Many veterans are returning to Vietnam to help rebuild the country we destroyed. Who is helping our war orphans in this country to heal their emotional wounds? No one. It is up to them to deal with their grief as best they can.

I'd like to build a monument in D.C. next to The Wall containing all the names of the Vietnam Veterans who committed suicide. And yet another one for all the children who lost their fathers in that war. Perhaps we could put their photos on it. I'd also like to find all the Vietnam widows still living in silence and invite them to begin talking about what it was like for them.

You see, if we could fully acknowledge all the wounds of that war, maybe we would stop engaging in such violence.

Your article minimized the impact of that war. Maybe some of the veterans were more vulnerable than others. Maybe the vulnerable ones are the veterans who are struggling with PTSD and all the related stress associated with trying to unsuccessfully bury that experience in their psyches. Maybe some of the vets living in quiet affluence have not had the time bombs living inside of them go off yet.

Because our culture denies death so deeply, I was not allowed or encouraged to grieve the loss of my husband. I was silenced. I silenced myself because I had no avenue for the expression of my grief. Now I have found one. I began writing about this process around the time of my daughter's wedding. Writing has been the container that holds my grief. I know the only way to heal this gaping chest wound in myself is to tell my story and feel the feelings I did not feel years ago when he died. I was too busy raising my child and trying to survive. When the dam broke and the tears began, I knew I could not ignore the issue any longer. The tears haven't stopped. I just write through them.

The day this article appeared in the paper, my phone started ringing and rang consistently for about three weeks. I received twenty-five calls from strangers thanking me for speaking up. They all had similar stories. They felt invisible and alone with their unresolved issues related to Vietnam. Other widows, parents of Vietnam vets, wives of vets, and several concerned citizens who appreciated being made aware of the issue of widows and children called to thank me. Veterans told me of the ghosts from their past which still haunt them, ghosts that have been with them since they returned from Vietnam.

The night my article was published, I had the following dream:

I was reading a newspaper which was so huge it covered the entire ceiling in my room. When I turned the page of this huge paper, I saw my article big and bold with the headline "Invisible Casualties of Vietnam." When I turned the page again, I saw a live scene in the desert with hundreds of people marching, some in wheelchairs, some on crutches, some with blank stares in their eyes and looks of desperation on their faces. Men, women and children were marching all in search of something – on a pilgrimage so to speak.

The multitudes of war wounded were being brought to my awareness.

Everywhere I went I identified myself as a Vietnam war widow.

Grief Denied

When I did, people began to tell me tragic stories about veteran friends who had killed themselves or had disappeared in the woods when they came home from the war, never to be seen or heard of again. The term coined for those vets was "bush vets." They never really came back from Vietnam – they still live in the bushes.

Because I had challenged one of the "veterans living in quiet affluence" mentioned in the article, he called me and we met at a cafe downtown for lunch. He looked like a Ken doll dressed in an expensive navy blue suit. He has an influential position in city government and one would never know of the physical and emotional scars he carries by looking at him. I got a sense of those scars as our conversation began. He immediately told me about two Vietnamese children he had killed, one of whom died in his arms.

"There isn't a day that goes by that I don't think of them. To this day, I can't bear to hear a child cry, I have to go comfort the crying child."

When I asked him about any symptoms of PTSD, he said,

"I refuse to let that war take anymore of my life."

I got a sense of this man's strong self-will. I wondered about the energy it must take to keep the memories suppressed. After two hours, he left – had to go back to work. I wondered if and when his time bomb would go off. I hoped nothing ever happened to any of his children.

I received another call from a veteran who was living in quiet affluence. We met at a Mexican restaurant, ordered our burritos and sat down to tell our stories to each other. Loud Spanish music was playing in the background. It was hard to hear.

He was the only company commander in Howard's battalion who survived. He was rather quiet and reserved but spoke briefly of some of his experiences, seeming to fit somewhere between the vets living in quiet affluence and those who had PTSD. He had survived but not really. Reading my article reminded him of a poem he wanted to share with me. While reading it out loud, he broke down in tears.

Most real men
hanging tough
in their early forties
would like the rest of us to think
they could really handle one more war
and two more women.
But I know better.

You have no more lies to tell.
I have no more dreams to believe.

I have seen it in your face
I am sure you have noticed it
in mine,
that thousand-yard stare
that does not look out
it looks in
at the unutterable
unalterable truth of our war.

Johnny's Song
Steve Mason

When we parted, we both expressed an interest in getting together again. He kept telling me how happy he was and how he had learned to love again. Yet in the next sentence he'd say how he was afraid of commitment and unable to make any long-term promises. I couldn't get a sense of who he was. It was as if there was nobody home.

I called him a few weeks later and left a message on his voice mail at work. I wanted to return the book of poetry he had lent me. He never returned my call. I guess I scared him away. I guess he didn't want to open his box of memories more than he already had.

A similar thing happened with a Vietnam widow. She called to say how excited she was to know there was another widow in her town. Her husband had died on the last day of his tour in Vietnam. She and her three small children were waiting for him to return when the Army vehicle pulled up instead to inform her of his death. We met for coffee and after two hours, she was ready to go. She expressed an interest in getting together again, and in becoming friends. After calling and leaving several messages, I gave up. She didn't return my calls.

It seems as if the experiences that we, the survivors of that war, have tried to forget, deny, and ignore are now knocking on the door of our consciousness, asking to be remembered and finally dealt with so that we can truly move forward with our lives.

One call I received was from a veteran who had been through four months of inpatient treatment for Post-Traumatic Stress Disorder at the Vet Center in Menlo Park, CA. He had two failed marriages and four children, none of whom he saw on a regular basis, although he was attempting to build a relationship with his oldest child.

People kept telling him something was wrong, but he refused to believe it. He continued to battle the inner demons until he went berserk, scared himself and went in for treatment. I met him two years after he left Menlo Park.

He called to thank me for writing the article. He had been a helicopter door gunner in Vietnam and was finally coming to terms with how his war experience had affected him. He had been unable to live with his wife and children since he returned from the war, but instead had stayed out in the woods repairing helicopters, and sending his paychecks home. When I met him he was 100% disabled with PTSD and could no longer work.

He showed me some of his slides he had taken in Vietnam. In one, Snoopy was painted on the side of his helicopter with the words, "Damn you, Charlie." (Charlie was the nickname for the enemy.)

Since leaving Menlo Park, he had been hospitalized twice in two years. The anniversary dates of his most traumatic time in Vietnam were difficult for him. His memories grew worse during those months. He had stopped drinking alcohol but had gained 100 pounds in the last year and was wondering how and why that had happened.

Grief Denied

One woman who was married to a Vietnam veteran called to say her husband was in denial about the impact the war had on him. She had learned about PTSD and was trying to convince him to seek treatment.

One father called to say he had two sons who went to Vietnam. "They weren't physically injured, but psychologically damaged," he told me.

I also received a note from a woman who lost her husband in the Korean Conflict. She spoke of the pain she and her daughter have lived with because of losing a husband and a father in a war that was even more denied than Vietnam. I invited her to meet with me, but she didn't respond. She said her daughter had three failed marriages in her attempts to find the daddy she never knew.

Expressing my feelings through the article opened the door for me to meet other prisoners of that war. I no longer felt so isolated and alone.

9. Continued Healing and Investigation

A week after my article was published, I got a call from a reporter at CNN wanting to interview me for a special they were doing about the real meaning of Memorial Day.

When I went to their studios in San Francisco, I took a photo album I had assembled for the presentations I'd been giving. One photo returned with Howard's personal effects was of him sitting on the ground, smiling as usual, holding three dogs on his lap. I found a similar photo of Michelle holding three puppies on her lap. I put the two photos side-by-side. The resemblance was striking.

CNN showed a few photos of Howard and me before he went to Vietnam and then, side-by-side, the photos of Howard in Vietnam with the dogs and Michelle with her puppies.

After the interview I called Howard's parents to tell them there was going to be a segment about their son on CNN. My mother-in-law had to hang up because she started crying. She called later and thanked me for doing the interview. She had called all their relatives and they had all seen the piece on CNN. It was the first public acknowledgement of the sacrifice their son had made so many years ago.

Grief Denied

A week later a flyer miraculously ended up in my hands about the existence of a writer's group for Vietnam veterans and their families. It was led by Maxine Hong Kingston and sponsored by the Community of Mindful Living in Berkeley, CA. The group gathered monthly for a day-long workshop.

When I went to my first gathering of this group, which was held on the Berkeley campus of the University of California, I had flashbacks to the campus of Southern Illinois University in the Spring of '70 when the students were threatening to burn the campus if the war in Vietnam continued. During our writing session, my anger flared up.

What they couldn't tell me when they came to my door that day –
what they couldn't say was

DEAD

They were telling me he was **DEAD**, *but they wouldn't say* **DEAD**.

GOD DAMN IT.......SAY IT.......DEAD...........DEAD

TELL ME...........HE'S DEAD.

AND TELL ME HOW MANY OTHERS

ARE DEAD.

THEY'RE   DEAD.

THEY'RE   GONE.

THEY'RE   NOT   COMING   BACK.

TELL   ME   THEY   ARE   DEAD.

HAVE   SOME   GUTS.

SAY   WHAT'S   HAPPENING   OVER   THERE.

PEOPLE   ARE   DYING.

SAY   IT.   SAY   IT.   SAY   IT.

A Vietnam Widow's Story

The military informed all those 58,196 families of the death of their loved one without even using the word dead.

Denial of death in our culture is deep. Fatally wounded or mortally wounded aren't clear enough words for me.

The audio tape I sent him on May 1, 1968 had a big red hand stamped on it with a finger pointing to the return address...

"Verified Deceased - Return to Sender"

And the message that came with his medals describing his actions on the day of his death...

"Completely disregarding his own safety, Sgt. Querry crossed the bla, bla bla...

Those words stab holes in my heart. Holes I can't fill up anymore. Those words that describe the scene of his death – they puncture holes in my heart. Those holes are wounds I've tried to deny for many years – wounds I tried to fill with alcohol, men, work and eventually food.

Now I stand naked in front of a mirror, having shed all my armor, and I bear witness to these wounds. I see them and I want everyone to see them –

> *to see what*
>> *that man,*
>>> *that war,*
>>>> *that government,*
>>>>> *that country did to me.*

Grief Denied

Once a month for the following three years I attended the Vietnam Veterans Writer's group. We sat in meditation, we wrote, we read and we listened to each other's war stories. I was grateful to learn about the war, honored to work with Maxine Hong Kingston and glad to find another place where I could express my grief.

In the process of laying my dead husband to rest, it became crucial to find out why his body wasn't viewable. Cindy Rheinheimer, one of the daughters I had met through Sons and Daughters In Touch, told me how to order Howard's Personnel Deceased File.

It took six months for it to arrive. The day I picked it up at the Post Office, my heart was pounding just as it was back in '68 when I received his box of personal affects.

"Do I dare open it right here in front of the Post Office or should I wait until I get home?"

I waited. When I finally opened it in my own home, I did so reluctantly, scanning each page – afraid of what I was going to find.

The first thing I came across was a letter from one of Howard's friends who worked at the Bank of Oak Brook with him back in '65. He was inquiring about how Howard's body was identified. There was a copy of the letter the Army had written to this friend informing him that such information could only be given to the next of kin.

Toward the end of the file, there was a diagram of the front side of a man's body, showing where the bullet had entered Howard's body, and another diagram of the backside, showing where it had exited. It entered at his right shoulder and came out the left side of his back.

One of the veterans in my writers group told me the bullets tumble once they enter the body, causing extensive damage to the internal organs.

The diagram showed he had abrasions on his forehead and skinslips on both wrists. On the same page were the words: Body: complete. Fingerprints taken.

I still had no idea why the body couldn't be viewed. There was one particular word in the file that disturbed me. "Mutilated" appeared several times. That word brought images to mind of his body being mutilated by the enemy. It was quite disturbing to consider that possibility.

At one of the VVA meetings I met a veteran who had been a photographer in the Army during the war. His job was to photograph the bodies of dead Americans to determine the impact each particular weapon had on the human body. When I introduced myself as a widow, he asked me when my husband had died and what mortuary he was in. When I told him Saigon in May of '68, he got very quiet and withdrew to a far corner of the room.

Later that evening, I approached him and asked about his job.

"The whole time I was there, I saw very few bodies that were whole. The condition of the body depended upon the weapon that was used on it."

"Howard was killed by a penetrating missile wound in the right shoulder," I told him.

"Chances are the whole upper portion of his body was gone."

"Were the bodies embalmed?" I asked.

"If it was possible, but sometimes there wasn't enough tissue intact to hold the embalming fluid. I assure you the remains of the men were treated with utmost respect."

From time to time, I got phone calls from veterans who had seen a copy of my article which had appeared in the local newspaper. Such was the case with Charlie Harootunian, who called one day from Boston to tell me he had received a copy of my article from a Vietnam vet friend who lives in Texas, who in turn, had received a copy of the article from James Rigler, who lives in Mill Valley, California.

Charlie said he had been volunteering at The Vietnam Veterans Memorial in D.C. for the past eight years. He had been a lieutenant in Vietnam, and had left in March of '68, about the time Howard arrived. He went to The Wall every chance he got. His job required that he travel extensively, so he often stopped at The Wall even if only for a couple of hours.

I told Charlie I was going through Howard's Personnel Deceased file and had some unanswered questions.

Somehow Charlie was able to locate a man who worked in the Casualty Department of the U.S. Army. Charlie called him about my investigation of Howard's remains. Charlie then suggested I contact this man myself and ask any questions I might have about the condition of Howard's body.

It took me several weeks to muster up the courage to call. My old friend denial was always there trying to lure me away from such matters. When I called he said that the reason Howard's body couldn't be viewed was because it had started to deteriorate. He said the skinslips on both of his wrists meant deterioration had started to occur. I didn't know if he was trying to appease me or if he was telling me the truth. The day I talked to this man, I sat down and wrote to Howard.

Howard:
I finally received your personnel deceased file. I held my breath as I opened it. I scanned the pages trying to find out how badly your body was damaged. I'm only able to read tiny bits at a time. Once a month, I take it out and read some more. I always see something I haven't seen before.

Today I took a big step and called a man who worked at the mortuary in Saigon. He knew what all those words meant that were used in your personnel deceased file.

Grief Denied

He assured me your body was whole and complete and that the reason your casket was marked "non-viewable" was because your body had started to deteriorate. He said that even if you were left out for a couple hours, because of the intense heat in Vietnam, that deterioration would occur. He kept trying to assure me that your body was whole. He was very helpful and answered any and all questions I had. I wondered how he could still be sane after working at the mortuary in Saigon for four years.

He told me that your body was shipped to Travis Air Force Base and then to Oakland Air Force Base where it was prepared for burial. I didn't know that. I assumed it came from Vietnam to St. Louis. How long was your body in Oakland? I don't know. What did they do to you there? I don't know. It's hard for me to let go of your body. I want to know that it was treated with respect.

He said maybe I was better off that I didn't view your body because if I'd done that, the memory I'd be left with would be that of a dead soldier instead of the man I knew and loved. But Howard, I wanted to see what war had done to your body. I'm tired of being protected. I want the truth. I want to see it up-close like your comrades did. It has taken me twenty-seven years to be able to ask these questions. Having this conversation about your body is important in order for me to accept the reality of your death.

My next mission was to find the men who were with Howard when he died. Back in '68, after Howard's death, I wrote to his company commander asking for information about the circumstances of his death. He responded by saying that Howard had died in the arms of one of his comrades, and he sent me the names of four or five men who knew Howard well. I corresponded with several of those men and was told by one that death came quickly, that they couldn't save him, and that he talked about his wife and unborn child all the time.

I continued corresponding with one of the men, Richard Tucker. He was Howard's radioman and was right beside him most of the time. When Richard returned from Vietnam in 1969, I went to visit him in Virginia. We spent many hours together over the course of a weekend, but neither one of us could bring up the subject of Vietnam or Howard's death. We were too scared, I guess. Throughout the years, I lost touch with Richard, thinking that I had put it all behind me.

John Sperry, a Board member of the Mobile Riverine Force Association, which is an association of men who served in the Delta area of Vietnam, helped me locate some of the men who knew Howard. John wrote a letter to each of them informing them that a widow of one of their comrades wanted to speak with them. John asked them to contact him if they were willing to talk to me. One man responded saying that he had put Vietnam behind him and didn't want to discuss it any more. The others didn't respond.

Another man who was instrumental in helping me locate men who knew Howard was Budd Russell. He has a locator service connecting men who went to the NCOC Academy at

Fort Benning. He found two men who had been in Howard's graduating class.

One called me and said he could remember names and faces, but couldn't put the two together. He said he'd look through his attic to see if he could find any photos of Howard. I never heard from him again.

When the other man called, we had a lengthy conversation about the NCOC training. It was then that I finally learned why Howard was having nightmares every night during the early months of our marriage. Even before going to the war, the intensity of the training to prepare him to be a squad leader was affecting him deeply.

Someone told me the Veterans Administration could sometimes help locate veterans because they had current addresses for men who had filed a claim with them. I wrote to my local VA office asking for help. I was told I could write letters to each man and the VA would forward them to their last known address. So I wrote to several of the men whose names I had received from Howard's company commander back in '68 after Howard's death.

About a month later, I received a call from the Veterans Administration in Virginia. Richard Tucker had called them shortly after receiving my letter. He informed them that he'd contact me within a few days.

When Richard's call came, I was nervous, of course. I'm sure he was too. I told him all about Michelle and brought him up-to-date on my life. He said he'd look through his things and send me any photos he had of Howard in Vietnam. Photos were nice, but I really wanted to have a conversation about Howard's death, so I asked.

He said that Howard had died instantly and that their platoon sergeant had been killed also within a few minutes. When Howard was killed a member of the squad had suggested that Richard take Howard's rifle or his ammunition. Richard replied, "I don't need them."

"It felt like a sacred thing not to take anything off his body. He was my leader and friend."

Richard proceeded to tell me his recollections of the time leading up to Howard's death.

When we left the French Fort for the city of Saigon, we were told that we had been chosen to be part of an honor guard for the Tet celebration in Saigon. We had to bring clean uniforms, have our shoes shined, clean our M-16s and be ready to stand honor guard the following day in Saigon. We thought it was great. We only patroled the Delta and were wet most of the time. We'd never been to the city of Saigon. We were helping the ARVN army and we were to stand guard with them to protect the city people in the event anything happened.

When we arrived in Saigon, we were staying in these nice houses in downtown Saigon near the Y Bridge which the French or wealthy Vietnamese had built and then abandoned that week for Tet. Maybe they knew something we didn't. There was food and even whiskey in the cabinets. You could see the river, the homes and buildings on the other side.

Grief Denied

In the middle of the night while many were sleeping, all hell broke loose. It was a complete ambush. The battle continued though most of the night and the next morning the Viet Cong had retreated across a bridge on the other side of the canal. Company C was ordered to cross the bridge and flank to the left. Almost all of those guys were killed, wounded or pinned down and then they sent us across to protect and allow Company C to retreat. We flanked to the right.

It was two to three minutes of a terrible decision someone made to run us across that bridge. They should have sent in air strikes instead of sending us directly into the enemy fire. Maybe C Company was too close to the enemy for that. The enemy fire was coming from about 200 feet in front of us. Two hundred feet behind us and the river, our men were firing at the enemy over our heads. It's likely some of our guys were probably killed or wounded by friendly fire.

You can imagine how we felt when Howard died and the platoon sergeant got killed a few minutes later. We were finally ordered to retreat and we drug our wounded out with us. At that point air strikes started – at last – against the enemy which were underground in bunkers.

It was at least a day before we got back in there to search and recover the bodies of the dead. During the fighting we were in water up to our necks and the conditions were hot and steamy.

The man went down fighting. It broke my heart. He was such a super person to everyone.

Richard sent me some photos taken in Vietnam. One photo was of Howard and Richard sitting on their bunk together. They were both smiling. It was good to see that they had some joyful moments in Vietnam. I could see a photo of a woman on a stand near their beds. It was of Richard's wife, Donna, who, like me, was waiting for her soldier's return.

A few months later I got a letter from Howard's second lieutenant. He told me his story of the time surrounding Howard's death. His recollection was sometimes different than Richard's, but I let the matter rest, knowing that each man's memory is affected by so many different things. I'm not surprised that the stories were recollected differently. After all, it had been nearly 30 years since the incident happened.

The lieutenant's letters were very informative and gave me more information about Howard's time in Vietnam.

He said, "Howard was a very quiet and intense person who was deeply concerned about what he and his squad were doing."

When Michelle read his letter, she said,

"Quiet and intense – that sounds like me."

I was grateful to have some closure about Howard's death. I then understood why his body wasn't viewable and I felt a great deal of compassion for him and all the men who went through such hell with him – all supposedly in the name of peace.

When I was in this period of deep mourning, my dreams became more vivid and meaningful than ever before. I started paying close attention to them.

Marion Woodman, Jungian analyst and author, says dreams are the quickest way to get to the inner world; they contain the unconscious knowledge of the past, the present and the future.

The most dramatic dream I had was of the wild, abandoned, little girl in the rafters. That dream startled me awake in the middle of the night and kept me awake for three days. It reflected the condition of my inner psyche which I found pretty disturbing. I knew I couldn't handle this Wild Child alone.

Another strong image which came to me in my dreams was the face of a frozen woman.

A young woman was alive and vital, but something terrible happened, which turned her to stone right before my eyes. When she was turned to stone, the expression on her face was one of extreme anguish and terror.

This image, I believe, was symbolic of my frozen feelings.

In yet another dream:

I was driving a motorcycle across the Golden Gate Bridge in San Francisco. There was a coffin attached to the motorcycle. I was in a big rush because the police were after me for transporting a dead body without a license. I was a messenger of death and had to hurry before

I got caught. Nobody wanted the message I was delivering, but it was my mission to deliver it regardless of whether it was wanted or not.

In the speaking and writing I've done about Vietnam, I often feel like a messenger of death. In a society that denies death, my story is an unpopular reminder that it does occur – unexpectedly and unannounced.

Michelle started having dreams about her father during this time also. One day she told me one of her dreams:

Howard's parents called to tell her that her dad was alive and they were bringing him to meet her. She called me and invited me to come over to be there when he came. Her grandparents told her they would call her back and let her know when they were coming. She got busy straightening her house for her dad's arrival. The grandparents never called. Her dad showed up alone.

I asked her what her father looked like and she said,

"He was short and fat."

"He told me the same thing he always told you in your dreams. He was living with another woman and didn't want to have anything to do with you. I felt sorry for you, Mom."

Michelle had another significant dream when she came with me to a writer's conference in San Diego. On Saturday evening she came to the coffee house to hear us read. This was my first public reading and I chose to read the piece I had written about being notified of Howard's death and the inability of the U.S. Army to use the word "dead". The piece was full of the unexpressed rage I had harbored for so long. For the first time she heard me expressing it out loud in public. She was uncomfortable during my reading.

After I finished she questioned me,

"Why were you screaming, Mom?"

I thought I had been reading, but her perception was that I was screaming. She was embarrassed.

In response to what Michelle said, I shrank in my seat. Within minutes several women came up, tapped me on the shoulder and thanked me. They thought it was a particularly powerful reading. They encouraged me to keep writing.

It was then that I realized how difficult it must be for Michelle to witness my rage. She had always seen a stoic, victimized mother. Now she was seeing a raging, angry mother, and it must have been very frightening for her. As soon as I finished my reading, she wanted to go back to the hotel.

The next morning I awoke early and not wanting to disturb her, went into the bathroom to write. An hour and a half later, I came out just as Michelle was beginning to wake up. I crawled back into bed and she told me her dream:

She and her dog, Kim, were out walking in the woods and stumbled upon a little dead girl. She was alarmed and didn't know if she should report it or just pretend she hadn't seen the dead girl.

"Kim and I were really scared, Mom."

In response to her dream, I immediately said without thinking,

"Oh, that little dead girl is you. It's that part of you that died when your daddy died. The only way to revive her is to begin to grieve for your dad."

As soon as this came out of my mouth, I was shocked. I wondered where it came from. It seemed to come through me, not from me. It was every bit as alarming for me as I'm sure it was for her.

In the next few moments, as we lay there in bed together, the armor of her grief cracked open a tiny bit. She became a little girl weeping for her dad – her bottom lip trembled, and she said,

"Mom, ever since I can remember, I've been so afraid someone I loved would die. I can't tell you how awful it's been to live like this."

I immediately felt a barricade come up inside me like an iron door shutting. I later realized it was a defense mechanism protecting me from her grief. I had more than enough of my own. I knew I couldn't start feeling hers. She didn't remain in those feelings very long. Soon she was up in the shower getting ready to go shopping.

In the second year of my grief, I had the following dream:

Howard came back from the war and just happened to be at a party where Michelle and I were. He was very ambivalent towards us. Later in the evening when I questioned the host as to where Howard was, he said, "He went to bed. He was tired and asked if he could use one of my bedrooms to spend the night."

I inquired about which bedroom he was in and walked into that room very slowly. I went up to his bed and gently touched his hand to wake him. He reared up startled and said "What's the matter?" I said, "Howard, I was hoping you'd come and spend the night at my house. I haven't seen you in so long."

He looked at me with a look of indifference and said, "The war has changed me. I'm not the same man you knew." I wandered out of the room and down the hall. The man I had known and loved really was gone. I didn't know the man he had become. He didn't want me to know him either.

I've heard similar stories from women whose husbands returned from Vietnam. So many souls were lost in that war, even some of the ones who returned home. We lost the American Dream in that war – the ideals we saw portrayed on *The Ozzie and Harriet Show* and *Leave It To Beaver*.

The War robbed us of our innocence – our ability to trust – to trust our country – our God and ourselves. At such a tender young age, we were exposed to horror. It hardened us. It made us grownups too soon. We had to get tough to cover up our injuries. It made us all suspicious of authority figures.

But the greatest damage of all was the loss of our souls – for a life without a soul is like a river that has run dry – it's bleak, barren and dusty.

For twenty-five years, I had recurring dreams in which Howard came back, knocked at my door and told me he hadn't really died, but had been living in Europe with another woman.

When I began grieving, this dream started to change. He came back, didn't mention another woman, but instead wanted to be with me and get to know me. We'd spend time together like we did when we first met. One night, we even kissed. We were getting acquainted again.

As my grieving progressed, the dream changed again. One night I had the following dream:

He came back from Vietnam and I was still living with my parents. We spent our days getting acquainted again very slowly. There was no baby, just he and I. He was sleeping in my brothers' bedroom, in the same bed where my brothers had slept when they were young boys. I was sleeping in my old bedroom just as I had as a little girl.

One night after spending a wonderful day together, he invited me to come into his bed and sleep with him. When I did he began to make love to me. He touched, kissed and caressed every part of me.

I'd never been made love to like that before. I'd awake in tears and fall back into the lovemaking again and again. Each time I'd awaken, I'd be sobbing, my pillow was wet. It continued all night long. The next day I walked around in a glow all day. Instead of coming back and rejecting me as he had done during the previous twenty-five years, he had finally come back and loved me completely and whole-heartedly.

I realized that dream was really about my relationship with myself. When he died, I rejected myself. I took responsibility for his death. I thought I had somehow caused it. It was my fault. I lived with a rejected self for years.

Now, in this dream I had embraced myself and absolved myself of his death. That dream changed my life.

In the second year of my grief I instinctively began to perform symbolic rituals of healing. I never planned these rituals – they just came out of me spontaneously.

By performing these rituals, I was essentially revisiting a previous experience in my life and completing and healing the matters that had been left incomplete.

The first ritual was the letter I wrote to Howard on the way home from the weekend with the Sons and Daughters in October of 1993. The letter just flowed out of me.

In writing that letter, I was resuming where we left off when he died. I was opening his coffin so I could say goodbye. It was the first communication I had with him in twenty-five years.

I think that when someone dies, our relationship with them doesn't end. It just gets frozen. Grieving is the process of completing our relationship with our loved one and saying goodbye. Even though I had waited twenty-five years it wasn't too late. I could do it now.

A Vietnam Widow's Story

The walk in the redwood forest with the audio tapes he sent from Vietnam was another ritual. Listening to the tapes made him real again so I could say goodbye. He was with me that day in the woods.

The ritual of expressing my anger at my war hero was a crucial step in my healing. By not expressing it, I had kept myself stuck in the first stage of grief, denial.

The most powerful ritual is my own self-care and nurturing. I've loved and cherished the Wild Child that appeared in my dreams. Two stuffed bears were the symbols I used to represent the Wild Child.

For my birthday in '91, Michelle gave me a small, white stuffed bear. Later that month, I bought a larger brown bear to give to a friend for Christmas. I took that brown bear in a pink plastic bag to his house for a Christmas gathering, but I couldn't bring myself to give it to him. Instead I brought it home and kept it.

The small white bear represented the feminine part of me, and the larger brown bear, the masculine side. So many times when I was overwhelmed with grief and sadness I held them, wrapped them in blankets and rocked them. They became the objects of my love and affection. I'd bring them into the bathroom with me when I took my long, hot bubble baths by candlelight. I slept with them every night. In the process of doing all this, I was healing myself.

If I awoke in the middle of the night with bad dreams, I'd grab the bears, hold them tightly, and assure them everything was going to be all right.

Grief Denied

In October of '93, I performed a ritual in which I married myself. I called it my "inner marriage". Michelle and I had gone to Mendocino, a small artist community on the California coast, to celebrate my 48th birthday. I brought my two bears, a photo of Howard, candles, flowers and a big mirror. I wanted to see myself as I pledged my love and commitment to myself. I asked Michelle to be my witness.

Mege Simpson was my mom's companion for eighteen years after my father died. He gave Mom a ring which she passed on to me after his death. He died as a result of being hit by a car while riding his motorcycle. He was 85 years old. I have very fond memories of him. He cared for me and showed an interest in my life. I chose his ring for my ceremony.

I took the ring to a jeweler and asked what it would cost to convert it into a women's ring. He said about $700. That was too much. A week later I went back and asked him if there was a cheaper way to do it. He said if I could find a ring from a catalogue he had, he could insert the diamonds into the ring and it would be less expensive. I looked through his catalogue, found a ring I liked and ordered it. I now had the ring for the ceremony I was planning.

I was nervous about doing this intimate ceremony in front of Michelle, but I told myself it would be all right – she wouldn't make fun of me. I was following my instincts when I was making these plans and gathering together all these things. Every time I got nervous about it, I assured myself it would be alright. My daughter would understand.

We drove to Mendocino Friday night and on the way we listened to some of our favorite music. We both belted out the songs that contained so many memories from the past. Saturday we shopped all day. I think we went to every shop in town. I was beat. When we got back to our lodge, all Michelle could do was lament because she hadn't brought her dog, Chuckie. The place where we stayed allowed dogs.

Meanwhile, I went into the bathroom to meditate. I took a couple cushions off the couch and stacked them up in the bathroom next to the shower stall and lit a candle. I do some of my best writing and meditating in the bathroom.

In the midst of meditating, as often happens, deep sadness welled up inside of me. I didn't know why I was crying, I just was. I was trying to cry quietly so as not to disturb Michelle, but when I heard a tap, tap, tap on the door, I wasn't surprised. Michelle asked,

"What's the matter, Mom?"

"Nothing. This happens sometimes when I meditate. I'll be out soon. I'm going to do the ceremony now."

I came out of the bathroom, gathered all my things for the ceremony and began. With Michelle as my witness, I, in my dirty turtleneck and my underwear, made vows to myself. I was embarrassed, but I kept going. It was a catharsis. I'd cry, blow my nose, say my vows, and cry some more – not at all like how I pictured this ceremony would be. I thought my daughter and I would both be dressed up and looking our best as if attending a typical wedding. Instead I was in my underwear, no make up, sobbing and sniffing.

Several times during this ritual Michelle wiped an occasional tear out of the corner of her eye, not really wanting to acknowledge she was crying, but not being able to fight back the tears. In this ceremony, I promised to stop betraying the Wild Child. I promised her I wouldn't put her aside or deny her feelings any longer. I picked her up, as dirty and unloved as she was, held her on my lap, embraced her and promised my allegiance to her. I promised to put her first in my life. Loving and embracing this wild, abandoned child has given me a new life.

Earlier that month, I had the following dream:

There was a deformed child that kept climbing on my lap calling me mommy. I kept pushing her away and telling her I was not her mommy. I was repulsed by this child. She had a sore in her left eye. She had oversized hips and when she jumped up on me and put her legs around my waist, I could feel the size of her hips. She appeared to be about 12 or 13, but emotionally she acted like a 4 or 5 year old.

That year, for my birthday, a very special Vietnam veteran friend gave me a lovely porcelain doll. I named her Beth. She had auburn hair cut in a bob, and real eyelashes. She wore a Victorian dress with white lace stockings and white patent leather shoes. She felt like a symbol of what I was becoming as a result of nurturing the wild abandoned child. I cried when I first laid eyes on her. I had never owned such a precious doll. Having her provided me with a lot of healing.

She became the symbol of the little girl I never got to be: sweet, fragile and breakable. I treated her with tender loving care. I put her on a shelf, but I didn't leave her there long. She soon joined the two bears in sleeping with me. Having her on the shelf reminded me how untouchable I'd been for years.

Another form of healing I engaged in was Authentic Movement. It is a unique form of self discovery. In the presence of a witness, with eyes closed, and a few creative props, such as blankets and pillows, one is invited to allow one's inner stirrings to come to expression through movement, sound or stillness. It is a sort of moving meditation, an invitation to explore and express our feelings like a young child does before words interfere. As the mover experiences being seen and accepted by the witness, she begins to see herself more fully, learning to trust her body, and allow her feelings and impulses to be expressed. New material emerges from the unconscious and the journey of self discovery unfolds.

In my beginning sessions of Authentic Movement, I did the same movement over and over again. I laid a bundle down at the feet of my witness and walked away in tears. I knew this movement had something to do with releasing. I was deep in tears every time. It felt like I was leaving myself – surrendering myself. I didn't think I could survive without this bundle. I think it was symbolic of letting go of Michelle and Howard.

In a later session of Authentic Movement, I wrapped myself head-to-toe in a wool blanket. I took Howard's photo into the blanket with me and held it close to my heart. I lay still, as if I were dead, with his photo on my heart. When the session was over, 45 minutes later, I felt as if I had gone into his body bag with him.

A week later, I marched in a Veterans Day parade with the San Rafael chapter of Vietnam Veterans of America. I wore Howard's uniform, displaying his purple heart and his two bronze stars. I waved at people, smiled, cried and identified myself in a very public forum as a war widow. I had my photo taken with Uncle Sam – the man who stole him away from me and never gave him back.

The following week, I wrote an article which was published in the Marin Independent Journal on Veterans Day. After describing my experience as a war widow, the article ends:

…Surrendering to my unresolved grief has been the greatest gift I have ever given myself. What I found in the process of healing is the 22-year-old maiden who married the man headed for Vietnam. She is alive and well and filled with hope. She is the one who marched in the Veterans Day parade.

As I heal this war wound, I approach forgiveness of my husband and my country for the tragedy of Vietnam. I take responsibility for the part I played in remaining silent all those years. I didn't have the courage to speak up then. Now I do.

Yes, Vietnam was a mistake – our country has made many. But rather than continuing to place blame, I set about the task of continual healing. As I do, I build a bridge for others to do the same. My bitterness and anger were valid responses to the hurt caused by his death. As I work through this anger, I find it now appropriate to work for peace within myself and within the world.

The dreams, the rituals and my time spent remembering and writing led me out of the darkness I'd lived in for so many years. Walking in the parade on Veterans Day was a big step, but the journey wasn't over yet.

Howard in Vietnam

Michelle in Middletown, CA

10. The Silence is Broken

The Vietnam Veterans Memorial Fund is a non-profit organization dedicated to furthering the positive effects of the Vietnam Veterans Memorial. Each Father's Day, volunteers from the organization honor requests to lay roses at The Wall in memory of deceased fathers.

When I heard about this service only a week before Father's Day in 1994, I quickly called Michelle and left a message on her answering machine telling her about it. I didn't know if she'd be interested, but I wanted her to have the information. I then forgot about it. She didn't mention it, nor did I.

A few days later I did a reading with the Vietnam Veterans Writer's Group at Cody's Bookstore in Berkeley. After the readings, a man came up to me and said,

"I was intrigued with your story. My mother was eight months pregnant with me when my father died in WWII."

I told him I thought he might benefit from contacting Sons and Daughters In Touch. He told me about a book he thought Michelle might enjoy. The title of the book was "Fathers and Daughters." The book contained photos of fathers and daughters along with the story of each relationship. I found the book at my local bookstore and bought it to give to Michelle on Father's Day.

Grief Denied

The following day while I was sitting at my desk writing, a strange event occurred. A message came. A message that was completely unrelated to what I was writing. I ignored it at first, but when it came a second time, I realized what it was so I quickly wrote it down. When I looked at what I had written, I was stunned.

I've had several of these incidents occur in the past few years, so I've coined a term for them – direct transmissions.

Earlier in the year when I was confused about what to do next, whether I should continue writing or do something that seemed more concrete and constructive, a message came... "God just wants you to write."

I posted it by my computer so I could refer to it when doubts crept in about whether I should continue writing.

I had begun to surrender and ask for guidance and it was being given. My skepticism was being replaced with strong, clear messages. It was unsettling at first, but I began to trust and allow these transmissions to occur.

Another transmission came one night when I was sitting at my meditation altar. I have a photo of Denise Laurent, my father's mother. She died in 1940, five years before I was born. I've always longed to know more about her. On this particular night I looked at her photo and asked for guidance. A few minutes later a message came. She told me that I was a third generation widow and that I carried the unresolved grief of the two previous generations as well as my own.

Denise's husband, John, died of cirrhosis of the liver when their children were all young. My father was only 15 years old. Their oldest child and only daughter, Addie, lost her husband also. She, like me, had been married less than a year when her husband died from blood poisoning. She never remarried.

The transmission I heard this day came from Howard. It was for Michelle.

> *I asked your mom*
> *to give you*
> *this book so you could*
> *begin to know*
> *in a gentle way*
> *what we both*
> *missed by*
> *not having each other.*
>
> *I love you*
> *my one and only*
> *little curtain climber,*
>
> *Your dad,*
> *Howard*

The words came to me without any conscious formulation on my part. I didn't seem to be involved at all except as a kind of medium. I had to believe it was Howard speaking through me – dictating a letter to his daughter. I fluctuated between thinking I was crazy or had just witnessed a miracle. I didn't know which to believe, but I couldn't ignore what had happened. I typed the message on a clean sheet of paper and placed it inside the front cover of the book about fathers and daughters.

I wrapped the book in exquisite wrapping paper and stuck it in my kitchen cabinet thinking,

"I'm not going to give it to Michelle. She'll think I'm crazy. "

Michelle was coming to spend Father's Day weekend with me because Scott was going rock climbing. When she arrived, I was, as always, delighted to see her. I particularly enjoyed it when she came to spend the night alone because it reminded me of the days when she was still living at home with me. She had only been at my apartment about an hour when this strong urge came to give her the book. I tried to ignore the urge, but it wouldn't go away. It came again.

"Give her the book now."

"I have a gift for you from someone special."

"Who?"

"Just open it, Michelle."

She opened the package and began leafing through the book with a puzzled look on her face. She finally asked,

"Who is it from?"

"Look inside the front page."

As she read the note from her dad, her bottom lip started trembling like a little girl's and she began to weep. When she cries about her father, her facial expression changes and she becomes very young.

Witnessing her tears broke my heart right in half. She only cried for about 30 seconds. She didn't say anything – she just wept. Then she put the book away and said,

"Let's go shopping, Mom."

The next day when she was gathering her things to go home, I started to help her pack. When I picked up the book to stick inside one of her bags. She said,

"No, I don't want the book packed with the other things."

When I walked her to the car, she put the book in the passenger seat right beside her as if it were a person. I could see the reverence with which she was treating it.

I was reminded of the visit we had made to Howard's grave just a few months earlier. Michelle, Scott and I had made a trip to Southern Illinois to celebrate my mother's 85th birthday. Michelle wanted Scott to meet Howard's brother, John, who lives in the Chicago area. During our return journey to my mom's house, we stopped in Springfield, Illinois, where Howard is buried in his family's plot at Oak Ridge Cemetery.

Grief Denied

I had barely stopped the car when Michelle jumped out and started running toward her father's grave – running – as if she was going to meet him there, but what she found instead was a tombstone with his name on it. She cried that day at the cemetery, but again didn't talk about her feelings. She rarely does. She just sheds a few tears and then wants to move on to the next thing.

A few days after I gave her the book, she mentioned that she had called the organization in D.C. and asked them to lay a rose by her father's name at The Wall on Father's Day. When she called, they asked,

"Whose name do you have on The Wall?"

"My father's."

"What's the message?" they asked.

Not expecting that request, she was caught off guard and said, "Happy Fathers Day, I love you. Michelle."

Michelle told me later,

"I was home alone when I called them and when I got off the phone, I cried for a few minutes."

That was her first acknowledgement that her father's name is on that memorial. It was also maybe the first communication she'd ever had with her dad.

"Happy Father's Day, I Love You." – a message left in front of a black granite wall in Washington – I believe Howard's spirit received her message and sent one back through me. I couldn't help but be humbled by this series of events.

It seemed as if the silence which had existed for all these years between Michelle and her father had been broken. As a friend of mine said,

"It just shows that there are infinite ways to communicate."

Several months later Michelle told me about a conversation she had with Lily Adams. Lily served in Vietnam as a nurse, and is currently a counselor at the San Francisco Vet Center. Lily told Michelle that deceased veterans of the war often speak to veterans who are about to kill themselves and ask them not to do it.

"Mom, how do you get dead people to start talking to you?"

"Well, first you have to believe it's possible and then you have to speak first," I said.

A month later on her 26th birthday, Michelle called me in tears. She had received a package from her Uncle John, Howard's brother.

When we visited Uncle John the previous Spring, Michelle had told him about what her dad said on one of the audio tapes he sent home from Vietnam – that he was planning to buy a teddy bear for her, but had decided to wait until his next pay check. She expressed her disappointment at not getting that teddy bear.

Grief Denied

Uncle John sent her a teddy bear for her birthday. Along with it, he had this note,

I know this teddy bear can't compare to the one you would have received from your dad, but when I heard you talking about the bear you never got from your dad, I had to go out and buy you one. Your dad would have been so proud of you.

It seemed as if Howard was whispering both in my ear and his brother's, asking us to give these gifts to Michelle on his behalf.

The book and the teddy bear occupy very special places in her heart and in her home.

11. Recovery of Self

During the the third year of my grief, I starting investigating graduate schools and taking the necessary steps to enroll. Graduate school had been in the back of my mind for fifteen years, but I'd never been able to take even the preliminary steps.

In releasing the grief, I felt lighter both physically and emotionally – like a new life was ahead of me – a life beyond being a Vietnam widow. I was interested in studying the relationship between creativity and healing. I had regained so much of myself through the process of writing, I wanted to learn more. The reservoirs of psychic energy that I had used all those years to suppress the grief could now be channeled into other endeavors.

I had lost 50 pounds and felt like a bird that had been let out of a cage after years of captivity. I'd often catch myself walking down the street singing, or being the one in a crowd who would say something uplifting and funny.

Years earlier I heard in a seminar that people who appear very solemn and serious often have unresolved grief. I knew that was true about me. Yes, I had always been the solemn one, the one who took life so seriously, but in the years of grieving my solemn attitude had gradually shifted toward light-heartedness.

A few years earlier when I took a computer class at my local junior college, I had a teacher who was always bright and bubbly. I hated her. I didn't understand how she could always be in such a good mood. I thought she was a fake and resented her for the joy which she always exuded.

Three years later, it occurred to me that maybe I appeared to others just as that woman had appeared to me, the happy, bubbly one. The cloud of grief under which I had lived was disappearing, and I could see blue sky again.

That year on July 6th, Howard's birthday, I spent the day at Two Rock Coast Guard Station in Petaluma. Earlier in the week, I'd been to Travis Air Force Base for my annual medical exam. One of the benefits of being a war widow is that the military gives you free medical care, but you have to go to a military base and see their doctors. If you live far enough away from a base, you can see a civilian doctor and get partial reimbursement.

When I was at Travis Air Force Base for my exam, they checked their computer and told me that I was no longer eligible for military medical benefits. According to their records, my husband retired from the Army in May of 1995 and on that day I lost my benefits. I had to laugh. The Army is still making clerical mistakes. They told me I had to visit the nearest military base with a copy of Howard's death certificate and my marriage license in order to get the records corrected. I didn't yell or get nasty with the employee at Travis when she told me this. I just chuckled and thought, oh well, I'll have to make a trip to Two Rock to get the correction made.

So a few days later, with his death certificate in one hand and our marriage license in the other, I drove to Two Rock to prove to the Army that he really was dead and not retired.

When I arrived, there were three people ahead of me. It turned out to be a two-hour wait. I went through various moods during those two hours – fluctuating between powerlessness, anger and then finally compassion.

The man who usually works in the I.D. office was out on emergency leave, and the two Petty Officers filling in were unfamiliar with the procedures, so everything was taking twice as long. One of the Petty Officers came out and apologized for the delay. I was gracious with her and even able to laugh and joke about the delay.

Since I hadn't anticipated a long wait, I didn't bring a book to read. So I grabbed the Coast Guard newspaper which I found in the waiting room. In it, I found an article written about a Navy captain who was soon to retire and had been a prisoner of war in Vietnam. I was impressed with his lack of bitterness regarding his experiences in the military. He had been a prisoner of war for eight months and his left thumb had been amputated without benefit of anesthesia.

The article said that when he was asked,

Grief Denied

"If you saw the meanest of your captors, what would you say to him?"

The captain responded,

"I think maybe I'd say, let me show you around. Let me show you what I was fighting for. This is what we believe in. This is why we put up with all your torture, because we had something worthwhile to fight for. Let me take you to Disneyland. Let me take you to a ball game. Let me show you all the wonderful things this country has."

The article continued,

"Any feelings of revenge?"

"Naah, not really. They are a product of their society just like we are of ours."

When my turn finally came, the two Petty Officers handled my request with efficiency, apologized again for the delay and wished me well. I walked away from the base that day noticing that my attitude toward the military had changed. I had a sense of humor and a little more tolerance for their clerical errors.

As I left Two Rock with the Navy Captain's words on my mind, I thought of that uniquely American holiday I had celebrated two days previously. Calistoga, the town where Michelle and Scott live, has a big parade on the 4th of July. Many of the locals go downtown at 6 a.m. and line their lawn chairs up in their favorite spot so when the parade starts at 11 a.m., they have their seats guaranteed.

Michelle invited me to the parade and asked me to meet her at Kelly's house. Kelly is her best friend and was maid of honor in her wedding. When I arrived everybody was all dressed up in red, white and blue. Kelly's husband, Steve, had American flags flying all around the house, inside and out.

Michelle looked especially stunning in a white knit top (the kind Marilyn Monroe used to wear in the fifties with her shoulders and back bare), blue-jean shorts, and her blond hair hanging in a ponytail out of the back of a white baseball cap with red stars embroidered on it. I was so proud of her. She always looks so cute, but that day she looked especially so. Her fingernails and toenails were painted red to match the stars on her baseball cap. She had on a red belt, carried a red purse and had little round sunglasses on. How sweet.

The minute I saw how cute she looked, I felt shabby. I didn't look nearly as sweet, sexy and all-American as she did. She was the belle of the ball that day.

I giggled and told her how cute she looked. She said,

"July 4th is my favorite holiday."

"Is it because you met Scott on that day?"

"No, I just love the 4th of July."

Then I thought – maybe it's because that holiday represents family, freedom, and main-stream America. It made sense that the holiday representing freedom would be so important to her. It's what her father gave his life for. I loved it that it meant so much to her.

12. Let Me Tell You About Her

Hi Howard,

I got the blues tonight. I don't know why. It may have something to do with the fact that it's the second anniversary of our daughter's wedding. Two years have already passed since I walked her down the aisle and she made a promise in front of God and all those guests – everybody except you. I wish you could have seen her.

I couldn't quite believe it was her, all grown up, doing such a grown-up thing – getting married. I remember all the years she came to me with skinned-up knees, or a broken heart over a fight she had with a friend. There was always something to cry about, and on her wedding day she was crying again – this time for joy. She found someone she wanted to make that promise to, you know, the one you and I made that beautiful Fall day back in '67, when we promised no matter what, we'd stay together.

I don't know how to begin to tell you about her and what she's meant to me. I know you remember that, initially, I wasn't too happy about being pregnant. But when you died, I was so glad I had part of you growing inside me. When she turned out to be a girl, I was even happier. I don't know how I could have raised a boy alone.

I didn't know you were going to die, Howard, did you? I wish we would have talked about it. One of your buddies, Bill Jones, who was in the NCOC Academy with you, said that they told you every day of your training that you were going to die in Vietnam. Why didn't we talk about it?

Scott, our son-in-law, never wants to come and visit at my house, because there's no father-in-law here. He gets bored when Michelle and I sit around and talk girl-talk. He's looking for you to watch the ball game and drink a beer with him. Where are you?

How can I tell you about all the years you've missed? Michelle looks exactly like you. When she was born, I thought I'd given birth to a new version of you. When people tell us she looks like me, she and I both laugh, because we both think she looks like you.

She wants to know about you now, more than ever before – about the father that never was – the father that only exists in the conversations people have with her about you.

I don't know how she'll heal from a loss that doesn't have a personality or an existence. At least I have memories of you.

She said to me the other day,

"Mom, I know what I want for my 30th birthday."

I laughed. She just turned 27 and she's already got her 30th birthday present picked out.

"You and Scott will have to go together and get it. It's pretty expensive."

That's how she handles it when she wants something really expensive. It's a ring with some special stone which costs about $500.00. She loves jewelry.

For her birthday a couple years ago, she wanted a Hamilton watch — she has expensive tastes just like you. The watch cost $350.00. I've never had such a watch myself, but I got one for her. I asked my mom to help me buy it. I'm not so sure I've done the right thing. Now she expects the same treatment from her husband.

The other day Michelle and I were in a department store looking for a pair of walking shoes. She found the pair she liked on display, but the clerk said they didn't have anymore in the back room that were her size. Michelle didn't give up. Before I knew what had occurred, Michelle said to me, "Do you know what she did, Mom?"

"No, what?"

"She took a pair of shoes that was on hold for someone else and she's selling them to me."

I had to laugh.

She usually gets what she wants in life — one way or another. She got the husband she wanted, and when she moved from Denver to California, it wasn't long before her two best friends moved out here also. I often tell her I wish she'd go to law school. She'd be a great lawyer. She'd win every case. She has the distinct skill of successful negotiation. Often when she's negotiating with me about something, I don't realize what's going on until she's gotten her way. I guess you might say she's slick but not in a nasty way. Scott knows her well and he's good for her because he's able to say "No" to her.

Her appearance is important to her. She likes to look good and feel good. One of the benefits of the health spa where she works is that she can get a free massage and facial once a month. She's not a tomboy like me. Her favorite pastime is looking through the fashion magazines.

I think Scott would prefer that she be a little more athletic. Once, when we were water skiing, he was giving her a hard time because she wouldn't try to get up on one ski. He was having difficulty getting up and she knew she couldn't, so she didn't want to try. She doesn't like to look bad or fail at anything. She's careful about that. She's a good basketball player. Even Scott says so. And she's a fast walker. When we're walking together she's often many steps ahead of me.

When Michelle called me the other day, I could hear an animal whining in the background. It was a puppy – a springer spaniel. She was visiting these puppies and called me so I could listen to one of them over the phone. She told me last week that when Kelly told her that she had baby skunks and a baby raccoon at her house, she dropped everything and ran over to see them.

She has a profound connection with animals, just like you did. She says the happiest days of her life were when she was raising two litters of pups. Doesn't that sound like something you'd love to do?

So, even though I don't have you, and haven't for many years, I have Michelle who has many of your qualities. She's slowly developing your sense of humor. She made me laugh last week when she came over to spend the night. She was staring at me, looking rather puzzled, when she asked out of the clear blue,

"Mom, did you get a boob job?"

I had to laugh.

"No, Michelle, I'm just wearing my padded bra today."

Ten minutes later, when we were talking about some problem she and Scott were having, she said,

"Well, Mom, do you think I should get a divorce?"

That's your kind of humor. I recognized it right away.

She's so tender-hearted — has much empathy and compassion for vulnerable things, whether it be an animal, a small child or a frail senior citizen. She's very passionate — constantly kissing her dog's nose, rubbing his ears, and hugging him. She'd do the same to Scott if she could get away with it, but he gets irritated when she rubs his ears too much.

As I said about her recently, "She loves what she loves very deeply — with her whole being."

13. An Only Child – A Surviving Spouse

Michelle has always been my confidante. Her father's untimely death contributed greatly to the depth of the bond between us.

Because of the conditions surrounding Michelle's birth, and the way my mother raised me, I leaned too heavily on Michelle to fulfill my emotional needs. Doing that denied her a childhood. When I read in my journals about the emotional responsibility she was already carrying at age nine, I'm heartbroken. She made it her job to keep me happy.

I spent most of my time trying to compensate for her father's death, trying to be both mom and dad – thinking I could repair the deep cut in the fabric of our family, if I just tried hard enough. Looking back now, I see that it would have been easier for her if I had not done that. My own unresolved grief was reflected in the way I spoke of her father and the circumstances surrounding his death. I was not proud, but ashamed. Everyone treated Michelle differently from other children which I think contributed to her strong desire to be normal. She was the recipient of all the unresolved loss people felt for her father.

Only now am I attempting to get to know and value her for who she is instead of seeing her as an extension of Howard. I wonder if she has felt that she had to live up to the expectations of her father. If so, what an impossible task. As she gets older, I think she is finally defining and designing herself apart from her father.

I believe that God sent Chuckie to Michelle to help her heal. Chuckie looks like a golden retriever but has the temperament of a labrador. He was one of the pups in the second litter that Scott's yellow lab had. Michelle gave away all the puppies out of that litter but the man she gave Chuckie to brought him back. He couldn't keep him. She has had him ever since. He is the smartest, most sensitive dog I've ever known. He adores Michelle. When we took him with us to Mendocino to celebrate my birthday one year, everyone who met him fell in love with him. It's easy to do. He is so gentle and well-behaved.

The Seafoam Lodge, where we stayed in Mendocino, caters to dogs. After we returned home, they sent Chuckie a letter inviting him to come back again sometime. When Michelle opened the letter, she told Chuckie to take it out to Scott and let Scott read it to him.

So Chuckie, envelope in his mouth, went outside to where Scott was trimming some trees and patiently waited for Scott to notice that he had something for him. When Scott took the letter and read it out loud, Chuckie sat and listened, wagging his tail.

Michelle was watching from the house – crying. I think she was witnessing, for just a brief moment, what she missed by not having a father. When she has her own kids and watches Scott father them, I think she'll mend her broken heart a little.

Recently when some friends had their first baby, she called me and said, "Mom, when I went to see Mitch and Sandy's baby at the hospital, I felt so sad. They seemed so happy, and I thought about how sad you must have felt when you had me all by yourself."

She said she was crying for me, but I think she was really crying for herself, and for the father who wasn't there when she was born.

A year-and-a-half after I attended my first gathering of Sons and Daughters In Touch, Michelle and I both received an invitation to attend a Father's Day celebration to be held in Sacramento, CA. When Michelle received hers, she called me the same day,

"Did you get an invitation to go to the Sons and Daughters meeting on Father's Day?

"Yes, but I don't know if I'm going. It's really for you."

"I'm going to mail in my registration today," she said.

I was surprised and answered, "I'll go if you want me to."

The Saturday before Father's Day I woke up very early. I was so excited that Michelle was going to a gathering where she would meet, for the first time, other kids, like herself, who had lost their fathers in Vietnam.

At 7:30 a.m. Michelle left a message on my answering machine to call her. I was out buying a Father's Day card for Scott from Chuckie. Since Chuckie isn't allowed in card shops, I do his card shopping for him.

When I called Michelle back, she said, "Mom, I got some bad news, guess what happened?"

I held my breath. I was afraid to ask.

"I'm sick. I've had diarrhea and I've been vomiting this morning. Chuckie got sprayed by a skunk and the smell was so strong it made me sick."

In the middle of the previous week Michelle had called me and asked me to call the organizer of the event to see if Chuckie could come to the weekend.

Cindy, the organizer, recommended I call the hotel to see if they allowed dogs. Luckily, they did. Michelle was thrilled to hear that. But now Chuckie couldn't go because he smelled like a skunk.

"Can you give him a bath in tomato juice?" I asked.

"Mom, I don't have any tomato juice."

I listened sympathetically, and wondered how the weekend was going to be if she had to leave Chuckie behind.

She called me an hour later saying that she had bathed him in vinegar and she was bringing him.

When we arrived in Sacramento, she was still feeling queasy. The program began with a picnic in the park where the California Vietnam Veterans Memorial is located. Michelle spread our blanket out under a tree while I went over to register and pick up my packet.

When I introduced Cindy, the organizer of the event, to Michelle, and Michelle told her how sick she felt, Cindy said, "That happened to me the first time I went to a gathering of Sons and Daughters."

Cindy then gathered all the daughters and brought them over to Michelle saying, "C'mon, I have a new daughter for you to meet."

I wasn't there when they all converged upon Michelle, but when I came back, Michelle was standing in a circle with the other daughters wiping her tears. Scott was lying on the blanket with Chuckie. I asked him if he felt left out. He shook his head, "No."

Later that day, Michelle told me she cried when one of the daughters told her that her mom was only eight weeks pregnant with her when her father was killed, and they don't even know if her father knew she existed. For Michelle that was a story that was even more tragic than her own. At least Howard knew she was on the way, although he didn't know she was a girl.

Father's Day holds a particular significance for these young adults. It's a day when their loss is painfully obvious. I never realized what it meant to Michelle until she called me on Father's Day three years ago and told me she was reading the letters her dad had written in Vietnam. She seemed joyful to be getting acquainted with the man who shaped her life so significantly.

Grief Denied

This Father's Day, we all gathered in Sacramento at the California Vietnam Veterans Memorial. The theme of the weekend was "Proud to Remember." Michelle participated in all the activities even though she felt lousy. She spoke to several of the daughters and sons and got acquainted.

We all went out to dinner in the evening and had a great time, laughing and telling each other our stories. I spoke with another widow who was attending her first gathering. Talking with her was like seeing a mirror image of myself. It was unnerving. Everything she said about her life and her dead husband could have easily come straight from my mouth.

She spoke of how she always idealized her dead husband, compared every man she met to him. None of the men measured up, of course. It sounded all too familiar.

Because Howard died so young, I didn't experience the day-to-day rigors of creating a relationship, the ups and downs of being married. I didn't live with him long enough to learn his faults. I've lived with the fantasy of how it was when we were young and madly in love. That fantasy has occupied my heart and prevented me from loving another. Focusing only on his positive aspects also enabled me to deny uncomfortable feelings like resentment, ambivalence, and guilt.

I'm trying to bury my war hero; to bury him so, perhaps, someday I can love another – one who is alive and perhaps not quite as perfect as I've made Howard out to be.

A Vietnam Widow's Story

After dinner we came back to a "sharing circle" where veterans, widows, sons and daughters and other interested people could sit and share. We started out by going around the circle telling who we were.

When Michelle's turn came, she said, "I'm Michelle Monhoff and my dad died in May of 1968."

Some of the kids gave the details of their father's death. One young woman wore a t-shirt with a big picture of her dad on it. Another had a photo of her dad slipped in the plastic cover of her name tag, covering up her name.

At the end of the evening, when we were on our way back to our rooms, we ran into two veterans from my local chapter of VVA. It was late – about 1:30 a.m. I introduced Michelle to them and she started talking about her relationship with me.

"All my life when my mom had boyfriends, I thought they were just a bother, but now that I'm married, I feel differently. Sometimes when Mom calls me and I don't get to return her call right away, I feel guilty."

I always suspected this was true, but this was the first time I actually heard Michelle verbalize her feelings of being responsible for me emotionally. It saddened me to realize that she still felt that way.

In the "sharing circle", when another widow was speaking about how she couldn't find anyone as perfect as her dead husband, Michelle rolled her eyes at me and said,

"You're like that too, Mom. None of the men you dated were ever good enough."

I was rather startled by that statement. But when I thought about it, there certainly did seem to be something wrong with all the men I dated. For one thing, if they didn't absolutely adore Michelle, I never spent much time with them.

Maybe it was easier to live with an ideal rather than a real person who had faults and shortcomings. Yet, what a lonely existence it is. You don't get touched very much.

Cindy asked Michelle and me to lay the wreath during the ceremony on Father's Day. As we laid the wreath they played the song, "Don't Forget My Daddy," written by Vietnam veteran, Jim Dixon and sung by his daughter, Janie Dixon. We kept our composure until we had walked back to our place behind the audience, then we both began to cry. As we stood there crying, several daughters came over to join us.

The speakers that day were inspiring. Glenn Rogers, editor of the California Zephyr, a VVA state newspaper, spoke about the angels that were with us that day. A son spoke of growing up without a father and the anger he felt at missing out on such an important relationship.

It was a very moving ceremony, much different than the one I attended a few weeks earlier on Memorial Day, which was all about dying for freedom and dying with honor – rhetoric that doesn't apply to the Vietnam war. The speakers at this Father's Day event were authentic and I appreciated that.

There is a great discrepancy between what speakers say at gatherings to commemorate the deceased war heros and my own personal feelings about war. I often want to stand up and scream,

"Give me the microphone, please, and let me tell you how it is to be a victim of war...there's nothing glorious about war."

As the weekend drew to a close, Michelle said her "goodbyes" and exchanged phone numbers with her new friends. I did the same with the widows I had met.

Then we headed back to our lives, feeling a little more pride and a little less shame about our connection to a man who died in the Vietnam War. Scott and Chuckie slept in the back seat all the way home.

14. Our Pilgrimage to The Wall

It's Fall again, 1995 and my life is very simple and quiet. Recently I went with Michelle to visit eight little springer spaniel puppies. It was a beautiful day and as we sat out under a shade tree and watched the puppies frolicking in the grass, I thought, "This is about as good as it gets." I wanted to take one of the puppies home with me, but I'm not ready for that yet. I still need all of my own loving attention.

On a hike with my walking buddies recently, when we came upon a knoll overlooking a beautiful valley, I started twirling around singing, *"The hills are alive with the sound of music."* I had to laugh at myself. That was unlikely behavior for me. I'm usually not so joyful.

In August of the third year of my grief, I went to an all-day workshop called "The Paradox of Love and Loss." I wanted to see if my tears were gone – if my time with grief was over.

I called my friend, Joseph, and invited him to come along. He had expressed an interest in the workshop and I was beginning to want to do things with people instead of by myself.

We packed our lunch and drove out along "D" street in Petaluma towards the coast. The golden hills of Sonoma County greeted us as we wound our way through them toward Spirit Rock Center in Woodacre.

Grief Denied

Eugene Cash began the day with a poem about a son who had died in the war. I was crying immediately. By the end of the day, I realized the completion of my grief was not really the issue. In grieving, I had opened my heart and with an open heart, I was feeling more than I had ever felt before. Almost everything moved me to tears.

I watched others cry that day and realized I had a new relationship with grief. It didn't scare me anymore. I could witness it without wanting to run.

And in the third year of my grief, I began to feel as if the process I was engaged in had taken on a life of its own. I was the main character in the drama, but I certainly wasn't directing the show. Incidents occurred which guided me toward what I needed to do to integrate the loss. Life kept asking me to open my heart wider and wider.

In August, my friend, Charlie Harootunian, who had introduced himself to me the previous January when he called to thank me for the article I had published about being a Vietnam widow, telephoned to offer Michelle and me a free trip to the Vietnam Veterans Memorial in Washington, D.C.

Charlie travels extensively for his job and had accumulated enough frequent flyer mileage for a trip to D.C. for both Michelle and me. I think it was 50,000 miles worth of credit he wanted to give us.

Charlie's very familiar with what happens when people come to The Wall. He's been volunteering there for years. He has a deep loyalty toward the deceased veterans and wants to be there for their families when they come to The Wall. The trip he was offering me, however, seemed a bit beyond the call of duty.

I was caught off-guard. I had to ask myself if I was emotionally ready to go to The Wall. I also wondered about accepting this gift from a man I'd never met in person and didn't really know that well.

My mind was racing as Charlie continued,

"I thought about it a great deal and tried to put it out of my mind, but it kept coming back to me."

Accepting his offer would be an opportunity for me to open my heart a little bit wider, and maybe by going, I could confront and complete Howard's death.

Michelle was ready and willing to go. She's much better at receiving than I am.

The following month I attended a two-day conference entitled, "Through the Broken Window – A Conference on Loss and Grief." I sat through the two days without a tear until the last event of the conference, when a panel of religious leaders gathered to speak about how each of their religious traditions deals with loss and grief.

I found myself drawn to the Buddhist nun who spoke about the time she had spent with her teacher when he was dying. After his death, she sat with his dead body for three days. When I heard that, I started crying and couldn't stop.

Grief Denied

Later I thought that possibly a trip to The Wall might be like that for me – like coming to Howard's funeral 28 years after his death and sitting with his dead body for three days. Except this time, I'd be able to express my feelings, rather than suppressing them as I'd done for years.

I accepted Charlie's offer to go to The Wall and found myself getting very busy again. I slipped back into the old defense mechanism to avoid the feelings that were beginning to surface.

The temp agency for which I worked offered me a month-long assignment to work full-time. I took it. After one month, they extended it another month. I worked the second month also.

As a writer, a meditator and a woman who has always been busy, I know that I need blank time – time when I'm not doing anything. Without it, I get cranky and irritable.

In October, the month before my scheduled pilgrimage to The Wall, I signed up for two weekend courses at my local university. That was too much for me. I should have been sitting and feeling the feelings that were bubbling up about this impending trip.

At the September meeting of the Vietnam Veterans Writers Group, Maxine announced that some North Vietnamese writers were coming to our October session to read from their work. I wanted to go, but the deepest part of me knew I needed to stay home. So I forced myself to stay home and I'm glad I did. Being alone with myself was like connecting with an old friend I hadn't seen in a long time.

A Vietnam Widow's Story

When Maxine told us the Vietnamese writers were coming to join us the following month, I had a reaction to their anticipated visit:

Maxine says next month some of the Vietnamese writers will be here in our midst. She says she hopes to have a woman who fought with the Viet Cong join us. When I hear this, I feel deep discomfort in my body.

The enemy, the people we warred against, have always been invisible, distant — in a far-away land. Now Maxine tells us next month they'll be here in our writing circle sharing their words with us. Our words and their words will be stirred together in the same soup bowl. Our war stories won't be separate anymore. How will we know who the enemy is?

I know in my deepest self this is true resolution and peace building, but my stomach churns at the thought of sitting face-to-face with the Viet Cong, the enemy, the people who killed my sweet husband.

Am I being asked to forgive, just as I was asked to forgive my country for the war in Southeast Asia?

Can I forgive the Viet Cong for defending themselves so fiercely, for murdering whatever was a threat to their way of life, their beliefs, their community — to forgive them for murdering my sweet husband who was waging war in their country?

You, the one who fired the bullet that took his life, what do you have to teach me? Rather than project blame on you for being the source of my sorrow, how can I own the enemy in me — the one who wants to destroy all beliefs different from my own? What can I learn about your way of life? How can we resolve our differences and live peace-fully on this precious planet?

Perhaps the beginning of resolution is listening deeply to each other's stories – listening with an open heart and an open mind – not judging what we hear.

To begin to understand how fiercely you fought, I only have to consider how I might respond to someone who came into my community and threatened my daughter, my home, my way of life. Might I not fight as fiercely as you to protect those things?

The paradox is that we were all fighting for the same thing – to protect our country, our freedom and our people.

We killed each other in the name of peace – we can't do that anymore.

I must end the war within me before I can be an apostle of peace. Otherwise I'm merely a hypocrite professing a philosophy I don't truly practice.

A month-and-a-half before I went to The Wall, I turned 50 and I told the temp agency I was taking a week off to go camping in the woods. I asked Michelle if I could borrow Chuckie so I wouldn't be afraid. After a few days, I sank into myself and didn't want to go home when the time came.

It was difficult to go back to my job at the mortgage company, but I forced myself to. I could feel my soul shrivel up as I walked into the building. I worked another month and then took a few days off before leaving for The Wall.

I allowed myself to stop being so busy and began to gather the items to take to Washington for Howard. Charlie told me visitors at The Wall often leave momentos. I knew immediately what I wanted to leave – the little pink dress which my mother had bought for Michelle to wear home from the hospital. I asked Michelle if she minded. She didn't.

I decided I'd leave the dress on a doll so I began to search for a used baby doll. A friend told me of a couple of shops that sold used children's toys, but I didn't find anything that suited me.

A recurring thought kept coming to me – *go to your favorite Salvation Army store – you'll find the doll there.* I ignored the message for about a week. When I finally went, sure enough, there was the perfect doll lying right on top of the stack of used toys. I picked her up and headed to the check-out counter. Everything was on sale that day for 50% off so I only paid $1.25 for her.

I brought her home, cleaned her up and cut her hair. As I did, I imbued her with a personality. She joined the two bears in sleeping with me every night. I kept telling her not to get too attached to living with us because she was going to be at The Wall for Veterans Day weekend and then she'd be stored in a warehouse with all the other artifacts that are left.

Within a few days I had fallen in love with this little, used doll. When I found her, I think she reminded me of The Wild Child in my dreams who was dirty, unkempt and needed some tender loving care. My heart broke open when I thought about leaving her behind at The Wall. I told my therapist about it and she said,

"Maybe you shouldn't leave her. It sounds to me like she's special and maybe you should keep her."

"She is special, but she has to sacrifice herself as part of this ritual. It's her destiny – that's why I bought her."

As I spoke these words it occurred to me that I was about to sacrifice the doll, just as I had sacrificed myself so many times before. I couldn't do it.

My decision not to leave the doll at The Wall was a turning point in my life. I felt certain, even then, that if I ever loved again, it wouldn't be at the expense of myself.

The Vietnam Veterans Memorial in Washington, D.C. is claimed by many to be the most sacred spot in America. It's a place where survivors of the war can come and grieve openly without shame and embarrassment. Few such places exist in our culture.

At the ground-breaking ceremony to begin construction of The Wall, Army Chaplain Max Sullivan said "May this be a holy place of healing for the conflicting emotions of that terrible, divisive war..."

A week before I went to The Wall, when I had gathered all the items I was going to leave for Howard, I fell to the floor sobbing.

The sobs consumed my whole body. I felt sure I'd fall apart at The Wall when I placed those items at his panel. I didn't care. I wasn't about to hide my grief any longer. Hiding it had cost me too much.

I also knew Charlie would be close by to pick up the pieces of me if I needed him to. Charlie began to feel like an ambassador of God who was taking care of all the details so I could fully grieve when I was there. I felt blessed to have such a sweet friend show up in my life with such a miraculous gift – a trip to The Wall.

The day before I left for Washington, several friends called to wish me well. Michelle and Scott came over for dinner that night. Michelle brought a photo of her dad when he was five years old and another photo of herself at the same age. The resemblance was striking. She photocopied the two images to leave at The Wall for her dad.

The minute we got on the plane, Michelle started wiping the tears from her cheeks. She said that each time she looked at the gift I was carrying for Howard, she cried. It was a stick I had found in the woods, to which I had attached an oak leaf, some feathers of a bird who had sacrificed its life and some beads I had made. Attached to the stick was the following poem by Rumi, a 13th century Sufi poet:

"The minute I heard my first love story, I started looking for you, not knowing how blind that was. Lovers don't finally meet each other someday, they're in each other all along."

Howard

Michelle

During our flight I showed Michelle the letter I had written to Howard. She read it slowly and cried a few tears. She told me that when she thought about composing a letter to her dad, she started crying and couldn't stop, so she hadn't written a letter.

Before we knew it, we were walking out of the plane about to meet Charlie and his wife, Ann, the two who had made the trip possible.

The night before we left California, Michelle asked me what Charlie looked like. I showed her a photo he had sent. As we were walking up the ramp towards the lobby of National Airport in D.C., Michelle said,

"I think I see him, Mom."

"Yes, that's him."

I instinctively threw both my hands up in the air and waved at Charlie. He gave me a big smile and, as soon as we were in the lobby, he walked right past Michelle and grabbed me and gave me a long hug. It felt so good to be welcomed like that. I then introduced him to Michelle and he hugged her. We made small talk about the weather and the flight and then he led us down to the baggage claim area to wait for our luggage. He then went to meet his wife, Ann Marie, who was flying in from Boston to be with us for the weekend.

A few minutes later he brought Ann Marie down to meet us. I giggled at their Boston accents.

Grief Denied

We headed for the hotel, where we dropped off our luggage, and then drove immediately to The Wall. When we arrived, it was getting dark. I was very apprehensive as we parked the car and began walking towards The Wall.

The Wall begins at ground level with the first panel being only a few inches high. Charlie walked with Michelle and I walked behind with Ann Marie as we descended down into the center of The Wall where the east and west panels meet. The panels got taller as we walked deeper into the earth – a descent into the dark soil that holds these precious men and women. When we reached the center of The Wall, we were in over our heads with the names of deceased veterans.

There was a silence that evening at The Wall – a silence I've never heard before or since. It was solemn. Many people were walking past the panels; most of them looked like veterans. They were so silent, as if they were walking past open coffins viewing the dead bodies of their comrades. It was unsettling. As I was walking I attempted to look at each name, imagining each one as someone with people who loved and missed them. I soon had to quit – it was overwhelming.

When we reached the midpoint of The Wall, Charlie explained that the first casualty was listed at the top of the east panel and butted up against it was the panel that contained the last casualty of the war. When we left the junction of the two panels, we started to walk towards Howard's panel. The Washington monument glowed in the background. I said to myself, "It won't be long now. We're getting close."

Just as I had that thought, I glanced at the row of panels on my left and his name jumped out at me. It <u>literally</u> jumped out at me. It seemed to jump off The Wall and extend itself out to welcome me – like in an animated movie where inanimate objects take form and move. I smiled. I felt I had just witnessed some of the magic I hear often happens at The Wall.

His name is on a panel that is only waist high. I knelt down to be at eye level with it. I rubbed my fingers back and forth over the inscription, up and down trying to feel him. Michelle did the same. We lingered for awhile and then walked around to see the Vietnam Women's Statue.

The Women's Statue contains three women in a circle. One of them, a nurse, is holding a wounded soldier. I asked Charlie if I could touch the statue. He said, "Sure."

So I gently touched the hands of the nurse. I touched the wounded soldier. I tried to feel their anguish. I couldn't begin to imagine their experience. As deep as my loss had been, I felt it paled in comparison to what the veterans and the nurses had experienced.

When we walked up to the tent where the books, t-shirts and posters were for sale, Michelle picked up the book, *"The Wall,*

Grief Denied

Images and Offerings From the Vietnam Veterans Memorial." She began to leaf through it. Then she handed it to me, open to a page, and nudged me to read it. Her eyes were filled with tears and she was speechless.

I responded, "I don't have my glasses, can you read it?"

She shook her head and handed the book to Ann. The image in the book was of a little girl standing at The Wall with both arms reached up doing a rubbing of a name. On the adjoining page was a veteran holding a small child on his shoulders. The child was leaning forward giving a kiss to The Wall. The passage read:

"Now I'm grown and I look a lot like you. Who would have known I would grow up to look like someone I never even knew."

It felt as if Howard's spirit was flying around tapping Michelle and me on our shoulders. I could feel his essence hovering around us there at The Wall. It made me smile.

After going out to dinner, we headed back to the hotel. It was getting late and tomorrow was to be a big day. Michelle and I didn't talk much, just drifted off to sleep.

I woke up at 2:30 a.m. in tears after a dream I couldn't remember. I tossed and turned and couldn't get back to sleep. So I finally got out of my warm bed, and went into the bathroom to write. Writing often empties my mind so I can go back to sleep. After an hour, I still wasn't sleepy so I took a bath, washed my hair, and meditated for 30 minutes.

By then it was almost daylight, so I went for a walk. I walked up and down the boulevard in front of our hotel. I was anxious. By 7 a.m. I was back in the room asking Michelle if she was ready to get up. "No, not yet, Mom. You kept me up all night with all the noise you were making."

"I'm sorry. I was so restless."

At 9 a.m. we met Charlie and Ann for breakfast in the hotel lobby. Then we were off to The Wall for the Veterans Day ceremonies. I brought all my offerings for Howard with me that morning.

As soon as we arrived at The Wall, Charlie checked in with the volunteers who asked him if he knew a Gold Star Wife who would like to lay the wreath for that organization. Many organizations provide wreaths to be placed at The Wall on Veterans Day. Charlie asked me if I'd like to lay the wreath for the Gold Star Wives.

When Michelle heard Charlie ask me to lay the wreath, she looked at me in a way that indicated it really wasn't what she wanted. I'm very familiar with that look. I hesitated for a minute and then realized I had to do what I thought was best for me. I told Charlie I'd lay the wreath. I think Michelle was disappointed that I wouldn't be sitting with her during the ceremonies. I didn't want to be on display that day, but I wanted to lay the wreath for Howard. I wanted him to see how proud I was of him.

Fifteen minutes later, Michelle came and told me she was going to lay a wreath. She had met another daughter with whom she had a lot in common and they, along with a son, were going to lay the wreath for The Sons and Daughters In Touch Program.

That morning I made my way to Howard's panel and laid down my offerings; my letter to him, Michelle's baby dress, a photo of Michelle and me on her wedding day, a poem I had written, and the stick with the feathers, beads and the Rumi poem. Charlie had brought plastic bags to put everything in, because it was threatening rain. He was right there every time I needed something.

I walked away and left my offerings to be viewed by the many people walking up and down The Wall. I didn't cry or fall apart when I laid my offerings down. I think I detached from my feelings because there were so many people there that morning.

Shortly afterwards I went to the kiosk to meet Charlie. He was going to be my escort when I laid the wreath. At the last minute a Gold Star Wife showed up and I told Charlie I didn't need to do it. He suggested we all do it, so I recruited another widow I'd met earlier to join us also.

I felt a sense of pride I've never felt before that day as I stood there in front of The Wall next to the wreath and next to the other two widows.

In the midst of the speeches it began to rain. Umbrellas went up, ponchos appeared and everything just continued. It always seems to rain on Veterans Day. I remembered the year before when I walked in the rain with the Vietnam Veterans of Marin County in their Veterans Day Parade. Who would have thought only one year later, I'd be at The Wall?

After the ceremony, Charlie and Ann Marie took Michelle and me over to meet Jan Scruggs, the Vietnam veteran who had the vision of building The Wall. I thanked him for his persistence in building the Memorial. We met Diane Evans, an Army nurse who served in Vietnam, and who was instrumental in building the Vietnam Women's Memorial. She was so touched when she met Michelle that she took the pin of the Women's Memorial which she was wearing off of her sweater and pinned it on Michelle.

Charlie introduced Michelle and me to many people that day; volunteers, veterans, and other widows. They all treated me like I was royalty. Never before had I ever been treated with such respect and admiration as I was that day at The Wall.

I was deeply touched by the volunteers at The Wall. They, like Charlie, have a deep connection to that memorial. I could see it in their eyes when I met them. They seem to know my sorrow and pain.

One of the daughters we met at The Wall invited us to have dinner with her and some friends at a Vietnamese restaurant that evening. We met veterans, widows and more sons and daughters.

Before breakfast the next morning, Michelle got up and wrote a letter to her dad. She introduced herself to him and told him that until she became an adult, she didn't realize what she had missed by not having a father. She said she hoped someday she'd have a daughter so she could watch her grow up with a daddy. She told Howard that I had been a great mom and that it had been difficult raising her. When she finished the letter, she said to me, "I didn't even cry, Mom."

After breakfast, we went to the Tomb of the Unknown Soldier. In the midst of the changing-of-the-guard ceremony, I began to sob. Charlie put both arms around me and held me as I cried. A man in uniform had just played taps and that had triggered memories of Howard's funeral.

After a few minutes we went to visit the Kennedy graves. Then we went to back to The Wall. There were many people walking up and down in front of the panels that cold November Sunday. It was so windy we had to secure our offerings to a wire frame that had been left from the day before. Michelle left her letter to her dad. She was ambivalent about having others read her letter. It was for her dad's eyes only. She did share her letter with Charlie and Ann Marie at breakfast.

After a short time at The Wall, Ann Marie and Michelle went to the car – they were cold. Charlie and I ran into Sandy, the daughter who had laid the wreath with Michelle the day before. We helped Sandy do a rubbing of her father's name which was so high she needed to use a ladder. Charlie and I held the ladder, as she climbed up to the top, so she could reach her dad's name. She recently found out she was pregnant, so she left a card for her father congratulating him on being a grandpa.

Ann and Michelle came back to look for Charlie and me. Then we met Diane, Sandy's mother. I invited her to come to Howard's panel to read my letter. It took her awhile to read it. She'd read a few lines, then put her head in her hands and weep, wipe the tears and begin reading again.

After she finished the letter, we hugged and I felt what I think the veterans must feel when they stand at The Wall embraced in each other's arms. I'd finally found someone who knew exactly what I'd been through. It was a sweet homecoming. We hugged and sobbed together for a few minutes. I didn't want to let go. It felt like I was hugging myself. She, like me, was pregnant when her husband died and had never remarried.

Before we left that day, Charlie took me by the hand and said,

"Come with me, I want you to meet a couple guys."

He led me to the panels which contained the names of two men in his company whom he had lost while serving as a lieutenant with an Army engineering company. His voice broke a little as told me the stories of these men and how they had died. Charlie expressed his regrets that these two men had died so young with so much of their lives unlived.

I told Charlie that I had read somewhere that when we fully grieve for someone, we embody their spirit. I suggested that maybe he had embodied the spirits of those men. Perhaps those men could live their lives through him.

The weekend came to a close much too soon, as I knew it would. Charlie and Ann flew back to their home near Boston on Sunday evening. When Charlie hugged me goodbye, my heart broke wide open. I told Charlie and Ann it felt like Howard had come home to me. He came home in each of the people I met. Although I didn't have him in the flesh, I had a sense of homecoming – a release that one feels when one is finally home safe, after a long, difficult journey.

Maybe it was "me" who came home that weekend. Maybe I finally came home to myself. I felt a sense of wholeness which I've never felt before. Something was different. I wasn't quite sure what. Maybe I had somehow finally recovered all those pieces of myself that had split apart when Howard died. I had survived a clinical depression and a journey into and through my grief – I had a lot to be thankful for. But there was more yet to come.

15. The Greatest Gift of All

When I got home from my trip to The Wall, I threw away the old moldy, cardboard box labeled "Vietnam." I took all the contents and put them in a clean, new, white plastic crate which sits right out in the open in the room where I write. I don't have to hide the remnants of Howard anymore. Exploring the contents of the box and giving my feelings expression relieved me physically and psychically of the grief I carried for years.

In December, a month after we returned from our trip to The Wall, the greatest gift of all came when Michelle called to tell me she was pregnant. She conceived a child the day after she returned from The Wall. I knew she had been trying to get pregnant for several months before we went to Washington. What I didn't know until a few months later was the request she made at The Wall.

One day when I asked her if she believed in God, she said,

"No, not really, Mom, but I'll tell you one thing; when I was standing at The Wall in front of my Dad's name, I asked him to help me get pregnant."

For the following nine months I watched Michelle go through her pregnancy. It was a difficult time for me. I was reliving my own. When the seventh month came, I was particularly nervous.

Grief Denied

Scott had a rock climbing trip planned for that month. I spoke to Michelle of my anxiety. She must have felt it too because she asked Scott to postpone the trip until after the baby was born. He did.

On August 11, 1996, after three days of continuous labor, Michelle gave birth to an eight-pound daughter, Alexis Madeline. Scott was there with her when Alexis was born. He cut the cord and both of them massaged her as she took her first breath.

Very early the following morning I went to the hospital to meet my new granddaughter. With balloons and flowers in hand I entered the room. When Michelle handed her to me, my heart opened wider than it ever has.

I've never before felt the kind of love I feel for Alexis. Perhaps because touching the depths of my sorrow has given me a greater capacity to love.

I make a point of seeing Alexis frequently. We play, sing, dance and simply delight in each other's presence. She is pure joy and around her, I have permission to be exuberant. She's teaching me how to live in the moment and how to let all of life in and cherish it.

I feel excited about my future and I know everything is working out just as it's supposed to. I don't have to try so hard anymore.

I know that whatever comes my way, it's all part of life unfolding, an unfolding which seems to include greater and greater experiences of joy.

Grief and joy come from the same place – the heart. When the avenue of expression is blocked, neither the grief nor the joy can get through. Grief, joy, sexuality, creativity and spirituality are all linked. Without all of these, we really have none of them.

I have a new-found faith. It's humbling to stand before the remainder of my life and realize that living in the presence of this faith is all there is to do. The measures I devised to manage and control my life almost killed me. Learning to surrender has given me a more joyful life than I've ever imagined possible.

Listening to my deepest instincts is how I practice this faith. The voice I hear when I am quiet and still is the directing force in my life. I think the Wild Child in my dreams led me to this Force. As I loved and cared for her, she guided me every step of the way.

Sometimes I call that Force the "Goddess" – sometimes I call it the "Universe" – and sometimes I even resort to that word I used in my childhood, "God."

Epilogue

Dear Howard:

I *t's Fall again, my favorite time of year, and it's the 30th anniversary of our marriage. This Fall is more beautiful than ever. I can finally see again – with the eyes of the woman I used to be – the woman you married.*

During the past five years, I've finally surrendered to my grief. I let it consume me, cleanse me, thaw my frozen heart, and teach me how to love again. The gifts of grieving have been many – the most precious being our granddaughter, Alexis Madeline.

It seems natural to speak to you now after having been silent for so many years. In recent years I have spoken to you in anger, in despair and in doubt. Now I speak to you in love.

I begin by saying I'm sorry. I'm sorry for holding you hostage for so many years. I'm sorry for blaming you and resenting you for the choices you made so many years ago. I'm sorry it took me so long to see the part I played in the drama of our lives.

I've blamed you, your parents, God, the Army, and our government for what happened to you in Vietnam.

Grief Denied

I kept myself chained to the God of my childhood in the same way, by blaming Him for your death. The grooves of anger and resentment were worn deep in my being. They've made wrinkles appear on my face. As I release them, I am regaining my youth.

For years I hid the remnants of you under beds and in closets thinking I could "disappear" you from my life. Losing you was the foundation upon which my life was built. That will never change. I no longer want it to.

Howard, thank you for planting that little seed in me before you went to war. You gave me something I could never have given myself... the experience of being a mother.

Being a mother taught me to love unconditionally and finally it taught me love's supreme lesson – how to let go of someone I love.

Thirty years ago when I marched down the aisle in a white dress on my father's arm, I felt pretty and innocent. When you died, I lost that innocence. In grieving, I've regained it. The breath that was knocked out of me when you died has returned.

It isn't easy to give up what has defined my life for so many years: Michelle, the grief, and you. I can no longer blame you or her for what life hasn't given me.

Though my association with you was brief (only a few short years) it has been the cornerstone of my life. We don't belong to each other anymore in the way we used to. The ties that bound me to you – my anger and resentment – are gone. The other tie, Michelle, is grown and married with her own family.

What binds me to you now is the memory of the love we had for each other. It transcends time and space. It cannot be severed by death. The twinkle in your eye, that I often saw, was ignited by the love in your heart. I cherish that love, always will and I'll remember that when I think of you.

I say "goodbye" now as I walk away from a life defined by your death to meet the life that awaits me around the next corner. Wish me luck, Howard.

Thanks for all you have taught me and given me.

I love you.

Pauline

To Order Additional Copies of This Book

Visit your local bookstore, or our website at
http://www.griefdenied.com

For autographed copies mail a check for $14.95
plus $3.50 shipping and handling to:

Pauline Laurent
211 A Stony Point Road
Santa Rosa, CA 95401

For quantity discounts, contact the publisher
by email at plaurent@griefdenied.com

~~For Credit Card Orders, Call 24-Hour (800) 852-489~~0.
*Please have your Visa, MasterCard, Discover,
American Express or debit card ready.*

Pauline is also available for speaking engagements,
workshops and individual consulting.